RETHINKING WHO I *really* AM

MARGARET BRISTOW

SM5OTH
S T O N E S

First published in Great Britain by 5 Smooth Stones Publishing UK

Unless otherwise indicated, Scripture quotations used in this book are from The New International Version, Copyright © 1978 by New York International Bible Society

Cover design concept by Phil Bristow
Design concept and development by Affi Luc Agbodo

A CIP catalogue record for this title is available from the British Library.
ISBN-10: 0-9563342-9-6
ISBN-13: 978-0-9563342-9-9

Printed in the United States of America.

Dedication

're-thinking who I really am' is dedicated to you the reader.

You are invited to take a journey in discovering afresh the truth of who you are.

Acknowledgments

I especially want to thank Phil my husband and best friend for being such a positive significant voice. I could not have done this without your patience and all our discussions.

Thank you too Claire and Michael, Rebecca and Dom for always encouraging me that 'I can do this' and for believing in me. You are the best daughters and sons-in-law!

To friends and family who have been there to cheer me on. Ann thank you for your faithfulness in reading and correcting grammar. Claire thank you so much for all your suggestions and editing, you have such a gift.

Affi Luc Agbodo and Jim Inkster, thank you once again for formatting the book and all your support, help and time given in helping to publish *'re-thinking who I really am'*.

Thank you.

A Journey of discovery for all...

As people we have the ability to be aware of ourselves and to place a value or measure of worth to 'self' or aspects of ourselves. We may use words like self-identity, self-image, self-perception, self-acceptance or self-esteem. All refer to the opinions we hold about the identity of self, the judgments we make about ourselves and the value we place on ourselves as individual people.

It is interesting to observe how people introduce themselves; a name will be given and is often followed by information about what that person does in life, the focus being on their potential for productivity. For example; "I am a nurse", "I am a teacher", "I work in retail", "I am unemployed", or "I am a student". The information given may also include ownership, the focus being on commodities. Information such as whether the person rents a house or has a mortgage, the type of car owned and increasingly the type of technological gadget/s in their current possession. It seems the dominant ideology of our culture is one of success.

As we are introduced to people, we can often find ourselves immediately making assessments and judgments about the person; and about our self-identity in comparison to what we hear. So often it seems that an individual's identity, sense of being, and perhaps worth is evaluated and defined under a criteria of life achievements and accomplishments, levels of productivity, and in this brand-name culture, by what commodities have been gathered.

I recently met someone who rather than just reply, "I am a teacher" replied; "I am a Head teacher", with emphasis placed on the role of headship. Immediately I knew there was importance for this person in the title, 'Head teacher'. As I listened to the reply, in my mind I asked myself questions: 'Was I to think more highly of the person because they were a Head teacher?'; Did their position add power and or value to their own sense of worth?'; 'Did their reply affect my own view of my 'self', and indeed did it alter how I behaved in response?'

I recall the early days of motherhood. As I met people in my new role as a mum the question was often asked: "What do you do?" The reply, "I'm a full time Mum" so often fell to the ground. It seemed as though my identity, my value, the thing that defined me, was determined by my role and what I did. After evaluation I was able to conclude that the things that employed my time explained a part of me, but did not define my intrinsic worth or the core of who I was. My husband suggested that I should play a game and tell people I was a child psychologist to test how differently people related to me. I was left with the question: in the perception of others, is occupation, productivity, and the ability to obtain commodities, the thing that determines a person's value, and indeed worth?

It appears that many believe that their identity is to be found in the things that they do and what they achieve in life; even from being a small child one is asked, "What do you want to be when you are older?" The difficulty with having identity enveloped in achievement is that the desire to accomplish can actually become life's driver; like a god that rules behaviour outcomes by dictating: 'If you want to do this then you must do..."'.

The concern is that the god of achievement only works as long as things progress well. What happens to the evaluation of 'self' when a 'crisis event' happens? A 'crisis event' may unfold when we can no longer achieve, or are unable to progress through circumstance. How do we view 'self' when we fail to achieve our goals or other people's expectations? How does our view of 'self' alter when we are no longer able to be productive due to life circumstances; unemployment, redundancy or sickness? How then do we answer the self-identity question, 'who am I?'

As I have lived and worked in various countries and differing cultures, I have observed the large role that family, or lack of family, plays in shaping the perceptions we form about 'self-identity'.' In the West in particular, we are increasingly motivated to trace our ancestry and uncover our family roots. By researching our genealogy we are seeking an answer to the important question: 'Where did we come from?' It is clear that our early beginnings have an effect on how we perceive self, others, the world and God.

Peter Scazzero and Warren Bird state: "Numerous external forces may shape us, but the family we have grown up in is the primary and, except in rare instances, the most powerful system that will shape and influence who we are." [1]

Beyond family, I have considered how much 'self-identity' is influenced by culture, social and political expectations and especially beliefs. For years I have counselled people

---

[1] The Emotionally Healthy Church: Chapter 6: Page 87: Principal 2: Break the

presenting with many and varied issues, and it has become increasingly apparent that underlying all the struggles in life is the key issue of how we perceive the identity of 'self'; and a need to address the 'who am I?' question. Popular psychology tends to use phrases such as self-image or self-esteem to describe issues surrounding identity. In agreement with the author Mark Driscoll I believe it is apparent that we all at times need to ask that far reaching, life shaping, belief revealing question: 'Who am I?' [2]

Have you ever questioned whether the value of an individual is decided and measured by ethnicity, beliefs, age, education or wealth? Other factors which may persuade your judgment are: family position, gender, and whether the individual is able bodied or disabled?

Consider exploring what it might mean to come from a privileged or under-privileged background and the effect that may have on the concept of self-evaluation and ultimately on behaviours. Ponder too, what effect it might have on an individual's self-evaluation not to know their parentage; or the effect of being born into a war torn, famine stricken nation. Were we to study the development of a person from 'the cradle to the grave' there would be a plethora of influential external factors that would affect self-evaluation.

However, whilst not diminishing the influence and importance of these personal, external factors, I have come to believe that all people are of intrinsic worth and importance

---

[2] Who Do You Think You Are? By Mark Driscoll

despite personal circumstance. Ultimately it is an individual's internal beliefs about 'self' that are key to creating a healthy identity and a positive evaluation of 'self'.

Ponder for a moment on the image of a small infant taking their first tentative steps in the big world, an infant commencing school, or an adolescent who is desperate to fit in and who is so often concerned about their image. Likewise, imagine a new university student who is leaving home and starting afresh away from parental figures; or the young adult starting their first full time work position; or a mother adjusting to her children leaving home. Consider an older adult facing retirement or an elderly widow or widower who is alone and has lived out most of their life. Throughout these distinctive life stages, each person continues the journey of discovering or re-evaluating self-identity and the answer to the question 'who am I?'

I have come to the conclusion that everyone, at various stages of life, is unsure how to answer the 'who am I?' question.

The truth is that because of the challenges faced on the journey of identity discovery we cannot be ignorant of the detrimental impact an imbalanced self-evaluation can have on individuals, families, the church and society. Our self-esteem and how we evaluate 'self', can take some real setbacks and for many this will affect our behavioural responses.

An imbalanced evaluation of 'self', from a low to overly high self-evaluation, can be hidden behind many facades. For example, an imbalance may lead to a negative and fearful engagement with life, or it may result in a determination to succeed no matter the cost. Some people may present themselves as successful and very achievement orientated with a self-esteem that appears high; observers are unlikely to detect that this maybe a façade to cover low self-esteem and masks the avoidance of pain, hurt and loss.

As individual Christians and as the family of God we are not exempt from times of self-doubt, or from seasons of low self-confidence. As a church it is important to recognise and acknowledge the struggles individuals have regarding self-esteem. We so often forget that Kingdom economics do not depend on anything we can *do!* Regardless of one's ethnicity, status, age, gender and achievements; the 'who am I?' question can present as a significant individual challenge to any believer and indeed to church leaders themselves.

As Christians, followers of Jesus, we are encouraged to engage with Jesus' commandment to "love your neighbour as yourself". It seems we take seriously loving our neighbour however the exhortation to learn to love oneself appears so often to be neglected or not understood. As we consider being a follower of Jesus, we must consider how being a 'child of God' alters the beliefs and evaluations we may have previously formed about our self-identity? How does knowing that you belong to God and that Father God knows you and loves you unconditionally, alter your evaluation of 'self' and the answer to the 'who am I' question? How does that truth alter your thinking and daily living activities?

In the Bible we discover Jesus' ministry on earth was all about his loving relationship with mankind and included healing the unwell both physically and mentally. We learn too, that Jesus was sure of his identity. He knew who He was and his ancestry. Jesus had a secure internal self-evaluation which was reflected in his immediate attachments, the way he related to others and explored the environment he was in. Jesus knew the answer to the 'who am I?' question.

I have come to firmly believe that no matter who we are, or what backgrounds or life experiences we have come from, that each one of us can be increasingly secure in our self-evaluation. I believe we come to know a deeper answer to the 'who am I?' question from knowing our secure base is formed from a place of relationship with God. In this place we can know more of God as our source, the centre of our being, and can hear the voice that speaks words of life and love. This is a place where we can be at home in God's presence. Knowing the greater truth of our identity is something that develops over time and is a journey that takes place as we know more of the truth of who we are as individuals in relationship to the Godhead.

're-thinking who I really am', is a journey of discovery for all: whether you have previously grappled with this topic, are currently pondering issues of self-identity, or are seeking to help your neighbour. The aim of the book is to provide modular stepping stones which enable you to be transformed by the renewing of your mind, to increasingly become secure in your true self-identity and so be able to answer with greater assurance the 'who am I?' question.

The modules will consider the origins of identity crisis and the source of a healthy self-evaluation, exploring what factors influence the development of a positive self-evaluation. We will discover how one's sense of 'self' may be harmed and will provide some suggestions of how to rebuild a true self-identity which may have become broken or distorted.

Margaret Bristow

Then you will know the truth and the truth will set you free.

John 8:32

Content

Introduction

're-thinking who I really am' has been written in modules. The book can be read by an individual or studied using it as a course work book by a small group or taught as a module course to a larger group.

The modules adopt the position that God is the source of our being. He is to be at the centre of our lives. Our chief goal in life is to glorify God and enjoy our relationship with him forever. He is God of the past, present and future.

As a life circumstance occurs or a narrative is told regarding our past, we each make appraisals, judgments and interpretations of that event or the told narrative, with resulting automatic thoughts (positive or negative).

Our thought life will then have an effect on our emotional, physiological and behavioural 'self' and indeed on our relationship with God and others. The choices we go on to make as a result of our appraisals will impact our relationship with God, self and others.

Although we cannot change our past, making changes to the way we evaluate or think about our past or a difficult life event can result in significant changes to our emotional and physiological well-being and our behavioural responses. We will refer to this process as renewing of the mind. Ultimately this re-thinking and re-evaluation, will have an impact on whether God stays at the centre of our lives and how we evaluate self and others.

Before commencing the modules it may be helpful to consider the effects of a distorted view of 'self,' whether that be a low to overly high self-evaluation and how it impacts an individual on a daily basis.

A distorted self-evaluation may result in:

- Distorted thoughts including self-doubts and self-criticism or being overly egotistical.

- Thoughts may focus on comparison of 'self' with others. Resulting in a harsh judging of the 'self' or putting others down in order to feel better about 'self'.

- An individual may have an erroneous view of how God perceives them individually.

- Low self-evaluation may cause consequential physical health difficulties such as persistent illness or chronic pain.

- It can affect behavioural responses resulting in possible avoidant behaviours and use of safety behaviours. Erroneous self-evaluation can be hidden behind various behaviours. Over time this change in behaviour will act as a vicious cycle increasing the low self-confidence.

- Issues surrounding self-esteem affect emotions, with possible feelings of guilt, shame, fear, anxiety and anger, and can cause a depressed mood.

- Over time people will adopt coping mechanisms, strategies, indeed habits that will be employed to mask the poor view of 'self'.

Although low self-esteem is not a diagnosed mental health problem, low self-esteem may be:

- Part of a presenting mental health problem, for example having a negative view of 'self' can be a symptom of diagnosed depression.

- It may be the consequence of a presenting problem, for example experiencing other psychological problems such as anxiety or panic attacks can undermine a person's self-esteem.

- It may be the cause of a presenting problem.

It is therefore necessary to note that while wanting to provide information regarding self-esteem, it is important to state that the diagnosis and treatment of associated mental illness such as depression, anxiety, panic attacks etc. does require the attention of a General Practitioner or properly qualified mental health professional. If in doubt do get checked out!

Symptoms of depression include:

- Increased or reduced appetite

- Feeling consistently sad, down, having a low mood

- Sleep disturbance

- Reduced pleasure in activities once enjoyed

- Poor concentration or difficulty making decisions

- Suicidal thoughts or thoughts of hurting oneself

- Feelings of guilt or worthlessness

- Restlessness or very slowed down in the speed of doing things

- Tiredness or loss of energy

If you or someone you are caring for have experienced five or more of these nine symptoms on most days for 2 weeks or more then you are advised to seek help from your doctor or a mental health professional. There are effective treatments for depression and research has shown that when depression is treated, low self-esteem is improved.

The information in these modules is not a substitute for proper diagnosis, treatment or provision of advice by appropriate health professionals. Do seek advice if you are unsure.

The modules are not a series of therapy sessions regarding self-identity; rather they have been developed to enable us to discover stepping stones which may help the reader to answer the 'self-identity: who am I' question.

Module 1

Laying the Foundations

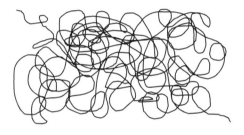

In our society the training of children already involves such threatening questions of existence according to which the meaning of life allegedly lies in rendering service, being useful and having purposes. 'Be good for something or you are good for nothing,' the beneficiaries of society are saying. When a man sees the meaning of life only in being useful and used, he necessarily gets caught in a crisis of living, when illness or sorrow makes everything including himself useless. [3]

---

[3] Theology & Joy by Jürgen Moltmann. Page 43(4)

I am fearfully and wonderfully made.

Psalm 139:14

Introduction

All journeys need a starting place, a station from which to depart. As part of an integrative approach to commencing the journey toward a healthy self-evaluation, it is important to lay some Biblical foundations from which to take the journey of recovery. This module will consider the five personal interconnecting areas that form the model of 'self' and will discuss the Biblical origins of identity crisis. The module will also encourage us to consider the significant voices that warred against Jesus' identity and will help us to understand the battle that takes place in our minds for our sense of 'self'.

The model of the 'Self'

The five self-esteem modules primarily integrate Biblical teaching and insights with some psychological theory and strategies, especially Cognitive Behavioural skills and tools. The modules are holistic and focus on five personal interconnecting areas of the 'self' that self-evaluation affects, each area is different and yet related:

- *Thoughts:* Self beliefs and thinking styles that may result in positive or negative thoughts about the 'self'.

- *Emotions:* The feeling 'self' that may result in positive or negative emotions such as fear, guilt, sadness, shame etc.

- *Spirit*: The essence of 'self' and one's personal relationship with God.

- *Physical:* The physical 'self' and one's physiological responses to circumstances.

- *Behavioural:* The behavioural 'self', what we do, how we act.

The model of 'self' can be drawn as a schematic diagram.

Model of the 'self':

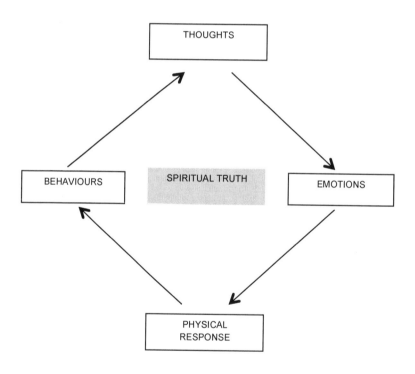

The modules take the stance that each individual is intrinsically important and of worth because they are made in the image of God. However as a result of early experiences and circumstances throughout life, individuals form core baseline beliefs about the 'self' that oppose and even argue against the truth of their intrinsic worth. These baseline beliefs are evidenced in our 'I am' statements.

For example consider the following:

I am unloveable

0%	10 %	20 %	30 %	40 %	50 %	60 %	70 %	80 %	90 %	100 %

I am insignificant

0%	10 %	20 %	30 %	40 %	50 %	60 %	70 %	80 %	90 %	100 %

I am insecure

0%	10 %	20 %	30 %	40 %	50 %	60 %	70 %	80 %	90 %	100 %

For each baseline 'I am' statement on the diagram an individual can rate their held self-belief from 0 – 100 %.

In order to protect and defend the 'self' from negative core baseline beliefs held about the 'self' (i.e. I am un-loveable: 60% belief) we each form conditional assumptions, and employ conditional rules for living. These conditional strategies ultimately affect our behaviours. We each adapt in order to defend the 'self' against the pain of being un-loveable, insignificant, and/or insecure. We each adopt coping mechanisms to anaesthetise against such emotional pain. For example:

If I do ...., then I will be loved.

"If I achieve well at work, then I will be noticed."

It is not the early experience or trauma itself but the appraisal and interpretation made by the individual about an event or told narrative about the 'self' that has helped form these core baseline beliefs. As children we have no ability to edit early experiences. So often the inference of a word or action or an absence of such will have led to the belief, 'I'm un-loveable,' 'I'm unworthy' or 'I'm of little value'.

The core baseline beliefs held by the individual about the 'self' and the appraisal of an event affect their automatic thoughts in a given situation and in turn influence emotional, physiological and behavioural responses. Indeed these beliefs and appraisals affect our perception of self, others and our relationship with God.

The Recovery Curve Diagram

The modules provide stepping stones that will enable the individual to take a recovery journey of re-thinking who they are in their relationship to 'self', others and especially in relation to their perception of God and their belief about how God sees them. The Recovery Curve diagram helps to describe some of the steps to be taken on the journey of 're-thinking identity: who I am'

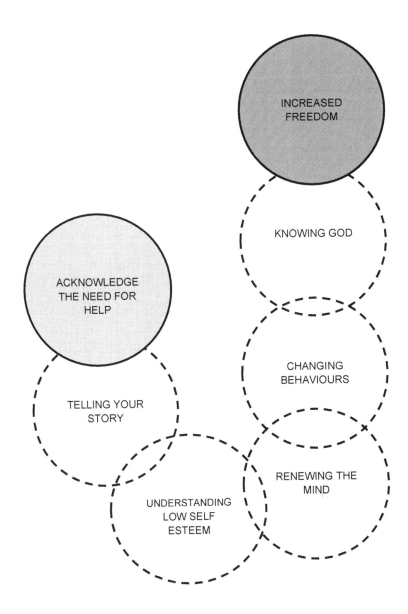

RECOVERY CURVE DIAGRAM

ACKNOWLEDGE THE NEED FOR HELP - It is important to know that it is okay to seek help regarding self-esteem and low self-confidence, and to acknowledge that low and even critical self-evaluation is significantly affecting daily living activities and relationships. It is also important to recognise that the core baseline beliefs we hold about 'self' are so often in argument and conflict to the truth that Father God holds about us. For example: You are precious and honoured and loved *instead of* unloveable

TELLING YOUR STORY – Desmond & Mpho Tutu in 'The Book of Forgiving'⁴ suggest that telling the facts of your story is how you begin to take back what was taken from your sense of self-dignity. They suggest that as you tell your story it is like putting pieces of a puzzle together. It is how we start to understand and make meaning out of our hurting. By telling your personal story related to your self-evaluation you are acknowledging to yourself that there is a problem with your self-perception. You will start to gain insight into the origin of your low self-evaluation and discover what is maintaining it.

UNDERSTANDING LOW SELF-ESTEEM – To tell your personal narrative to someone helps break the denial and perhaps secrecy about your low self-evaluation. Prayerfully talking to God about how low self-esteem affects daily life and relationships enables you to start to consider the consequences of negative thinking on your emotions, physiological and behaviour responses and indeed your relationship with God.

---

[4] The Book of Forgiving by Desmond & MphoTutu

RENEWING THE MIND – Awareness of how we think is a key to our self-esteem.

'Be careful how you think, your life is shaped by your thoughts.' *Proverbs 4:23 (Good News Translation)*

It is important to learn to identify our negative thinking and to commence the renewing / re-thinking process by changing our negative thinking for truthful thinking. This will include Biblical truths of how God perceives our identity.

CHANGING OUR BEHAVIOURS – When we have poor self-esteem we knowingly and sometimes unknowingly self-sabotage opportunities or relationships by using avoidant and safety behaviours to try and protect ourselves from hurt. This maintains the cycle of low self-esteem.

KNOWING GOD – A healthy self-esteem depends on our knowledge of how God perceives us. He is the source of our identity, providing a sense of 'self' and healthy well-being. A healthy self-esteem is the assurance of our significance.

'You are precious and honoured in my sight, and because I love you.' *Isaiah 43:4*

INCREASED FREEDOM – This is a process of re-thinking, renewing and restoration, hence the recovery curve. It is a life long journey as we negotiate each life stage with the assurance of how a loving God perceives the one he has made in his likeness.

The modules will enable significant recovery steps to be taken in understanding the concept of self-identity and help individuals to answer the personal question we each ask at various stages of life: 'who am I?'; In order to understand the concept of 'who I am' it is important to consider when and how the origins of identity crisis commenced.

The origins of Identity Crisis

When talking of identity western culture uses words like self-image, self-concept or self-esteem. How we perceive ourselves forms part of our identity; it is what we believe about 'self' that influences how we behave.

It therefore follows that to increasingly know the truth about our identity, changes how we evaluate 'self'. This self-appraisal influences how we think, feel and behave. It changes everything!

In Genesis 1:26 it says, 'Let us make man in our image, in our likeness,' it goes on to say: 'So God created man in his own image, in the image of God he created him; male and female he created them.'

We humans have the unique privilege of being created to image God. We are to be God reflectors. As humans we were created by God to reflect him to each other, as in a mirror. We were created to know ourselves in relation to God and one another.

This involves having thoughts and beliefs about 'self' that line up with the Biblical truths of our image in God. We are to feel emotions as God does and see them reflected in our behaviours; such as loving our neighbour, hating injustice and hating the effects of sin's destructive ways. We are to behave with acts of kindness and generous service within a community, so mirroring a Trinitarian God. In short we were intended to reflect who God is. We were originally made in his likeness. That is the source of our true identity.

So when did the identity crisis begin? The human state of identity crisis commenced as God's enemy, our adversary Satan, tempted Adam and Eve via the serpent. Adam and Eve listened to a voice other than God's. They were tempted and deceived into believing a lie. They chose to base their identity upon what Satan was saying to them rather than believing that they were like God because they were already made in his likeness. *Genesis 3:5*

'You will become just like God, knowing everything, both good and evil.'

This resulted in Adam and Eve being separated from God's presence. They moved from God consciousness into self-consciousness, creating their identity, their self-evaluation, as separate from God. They became incomplete. The first sin, choosing not to listen to God's voice, challenged man's identity status.

The consequences of Adam's and Eve's choices brought about a change at the core of their being. Their choices not only harmed their relationship with God, causing them to become spiritual orphans, but also with each other and for the first time their understanding of 'self' was harmed.

They were no longer God-centered. Note how each of their behaviours altered; they go into hiding from God. This is the first display of avoidant human behaviour. Adam and Eve experienced their first conflict/ disharmony, with each other, evidenced by a blame culture. As Adam moves to blame Eve, she takes on the responsibility of the event.

The consequential emotions are shame and fear for the first time. Fear separates us from God's love. Separation as a result of wrong choices creates loneliness because we are separated from our completeness in God's love.

Adam and Eve experienced inner conflict, no longer at peace with God or within themselves. Rather than listen to God's voice Adam and Eve chose to listen to the voice of a significant other; Satan.

When Adam and Eve listened to Satan their identity, their image, their self-evaluation, was tarnished and became distorted and damaged. They became separated from God, becoming orphans due to their choices. *Genesis 3*

Evil brings separation from God as Father, the One to whom we belong. It also brings separation from one another and all creation. Psychologically, evil brings an internal separation, an internal sense of disharmony evidenced by an internal 'dis–ease'. The identity issue is now about: 'to whom do I belong, who am I'?

'Orphan' means, 'separated from Father'. As an alternative to being satisfied primarily through relationship with God, mankind sought and now seeks to find love and approval elsewhere – often separate from God. As a result of Adam's and Eve's choice, all future generations would also listen to the voices of a fallen world. Not listening to God's voice meant that our world was separated from him, resulting in disobedience and our becoming 'slaves' to the voices of the world. The visible symptoms or behavioural signs of an orphaned heart can be hiding, mistrust, misinterpretation, poor attachments, manipulation, and a sense of independence, 'I must look after myself.'

The consequence of seeking false satisfaction and completeness in things other than relationship with God means that we fluctuate in our self-evaluation and our sense of completeness depending on our life experience in the world. The more we search for love and affirmation 'here and there' the more we give power and authority to the significant voices of the world.

These significant voices may be our parents, friends, teachers, peers, colleagues, authority figures and the media. (Note some will have definitely been positive voices while others will have had a significantly negative influence.)

As children we observe and experience life with an inability to edit what is being said; a child will believe that a parent or adult figure in a given situation is in the right, and therefore that they as the child must be at fault.

Dr. Robert Mc Gee states, "Not everyone goes through severe trauma of abuse, abandonment, or gross neglect. But many fathers," [*and mothers*] "nibble around the edges of these faults, perhaps leaving tiny bite marks in the spirit of their children rather than gaping holes of emptiness." (The words in italics are added)

This leads to wounds of the heart and children receive messages that strike to the core of 'self' identity – often only realised in adulthood.

It is noteworthy too, that most of us develop concepts about God from our early experiences, and these feelings and experiences also become intertwined and confused. This can result in a distorted image of God. Some may struggle with relating to God as Father, relating more easily to Jesus or the Holy Spirit. This will be largely because of difficulties with earthly fathers or father figures.

Distorted images of God may be; seeing Father God as authoritarian; disinterested; emotionally distant; unreliable or even as abusive.

For example, children or teenagers who experience an absent parent due to work, separation, divorce, the premature death of a parent or prolonged absence, will struggle with their security. This may manifest with possible feelings of rejection, hurt, loss and anger, and some will have come to believe they are to blame for the absence. This in turn will affect their image of God as Father.

CASE EXAMPLE - Lucy

Lucy's father had an affair and left home when she was 5 years old. He was a good man and tried to see her and her siblings often. The message that settled in her heart as a teenage girl was, 'You better do more than she (mother) did or you won't be able to sustain a relationship.'

'He chose to live with his other children; I must be faulty.' (I'm un-likeable)

As Lucy became an adult she constantly changed her behaviour to please her partner and lived with an underlying fear that there was something wrong with her. She felt that she didn't belong and that she was faulty in some way. She told her 'self':

'If I had been better he (father) would have loved us and longed to be with us. He would have fought for us. It must be me.'

CASE EXAMPLE – David

David was the eldest of four siblings. His father was very authoritarian and ruled the home with strict rules of discipline. There was little money and his father worked long hours at a factory including Saturday and Sunday mornings; in the evening he would do part-time work to supplement the wages. When he was present he was silent or reading the newspaper with little conversation or words of affirmation.

David grew up afraid of his father and saw him as emotionally distant. David grew up not feeling heard by his father or having his feelings validated or acknowledged. He was regularly told, 'don't be silly', 'boys don't cry'.

As an adult he became ashamed of his emotions, not understanding his own feelings or his anger toward his father, believing, and 'I shouldn't feel like this, I must be bad.'

As we explore the significant voices and messages received during early life experiences, consider the child who repeatedly, without positive affirmation, hears:

'*You will never amount to much*'

'*You are so stupid*'

'*You will never be like your brother/sister*'

'After all I have done for you'

'You should work harder'

Such a child will long for significance and acceptance and will seek to be loved in many and varied places. For example they may seek significance and security through possessions, work achievement and status in society.

This ultimately 'ties us up', and places us in bondage (slavery) to fear and anxiety because the voices of the world are conditional, 'if you do ..., then such and such will happen'. Indeed we enter a system of works (productivity) in order to find significance, security and acceptance.

For example 'If you do ..., then I will love you'. 'If you work and achieve ..., then I will reward you with affirmation.' This conditional rewarding 'hooks us in' to relationships and circumstances but will never satisfy the deepest longing of the human heart: to be loved unconditionally, to be significant, secure and accepted in relationship with our creator God, whose unconditional love is a free gift.

Consider the story of the Prodigal son. The younger son had all he needed, just like Adam and Eve, but he chose to leave home. The son rejected the values of his family and journeyed to a distant land in defiant rebellion to his father. Imagine the Father's deep grief as he gave his son choices, just as Father God did with Adam and Eve and still does with each individual. God will never take away our free will to make choices.

Just as Adam and Eve listened to the voice of a significant other, in the same way the prodigal son made choices to leave home. The seductive voice of promise and hope of affirmation and success elsewhere called to him to go and discover himself separate from his family and from God.

Likewise, we often go somewhere other than God to search for love, significance, security, and acceptance. As individuals we too can feel the need to prove we are worth loving by being part of the crowd and by achieving success. In the steps of the Prodigal son, we often become deaf to the very voice that calls us chosen and loved. We have also listened to the significant voices of the world; some will have been positive, but those of negative influence will have wooed us to turn away from a loving relationship with God.

Rather than having listened to the truth that God has to say about who we are in Christ, each of us at various times have been deceived and tempted to listen to the voice/s of significant others in our lives concerning the truth about our identity. We will all have made interpretations and appraisals that tell us 'you are not accepted and loved until you ... '

As children we also may have made vows that shut our hearts down. John and Stasi Eldredge in their book 'Captivating' describe how vows are "a deep-seated agreement with the message of our wounds. They act as an agreement with the verdict on us". [5]

For instance: 'Fine. I will live my life in the following way...'

The voices of the world and of significant others can cause us to have doubts about our value and worth. The consequence

---

[5] Captivating by John & Stasi Eldredge: page 70

of listening to alternative voices, messages that shape our lives and of making vows, is an altering of our behaviours. We modify our behaviour in order to seek approval and affirmation from others, to feel significant, to protect our 'self' from perceived danger and to anaesthetise our hearts from pain. These are self-protective behaviours.

A result of having believed these lies about personal value and self-worth is that many people have wounded hearts and will have lost sight of the truth of their significance and worth in relation to God. This will have tarnished and distorted the evaluation of 'self' and for some will have significantly lowered self-esteem.

Exercise Task 1

Make a note of the significant voices / messages you have listened to in the past:

Remember that it is also sometimes the absence of a longed for, positive voice that can also influence our self-evaluation.

Significant voices / messages that have positively influenced your self-esteem/evaluation:

....

....

....

....

....

Significant voices / messages that have negatively influenced your self-esteem/evaluation:

....
....
....
....
....

Significant voices that were absent (a longed for positive voice) that has influenced your self-esteem/evaluation:

....
....
....
....
....

Most of us develop concepts about God from our early experiences. What messages informed your concept of God?

....
....
....
....
....

If you find it difficult to recall these significant voices, ask God to help you remember. Also, consider speaking with someone you trust who can help you explore the past: perhaps a sibling or long standing friend.

The hope is that as we take steps to encourage a healthy self-esteem, and to discover more of our true identity in Christ, we will see a restoration of the God-like image we are called to reflect and gain a right understanding of who Father God is.

The recovery journey of knowing more of your true identity will involve moving:

From *Identity crisis*

To *Identity completeness*

Reunion = Relationship with God head + listening to and Knowing God + renewing of our minds + renewed 'self' identity + renewed relationships with others.

The truth is that none of us can change our past and we don't know our future but we can learn to re-think who we are. This is truly possible as we find our self-esteem, our identity, in the God who so loved the world that he sent Jesus to us to redeem our self-identity, to redeem our old 'self'. God has made us in his image and so loved us that he made a way for believers in Christ to be adopted and brought back into the family of God. We are made complete and made whole in Christ as we live in his presence.

Our minds are a battle field

A result of having believed these lies about personal value and self-worth is that many will have lost sight of the truth of their significance and worth. This will often be reflected in self-critical judgments and personal self-talk. Consider for a moment, on a day to day basis how you view yourself personally, what is the content of your personal self-talk.

Who do you say you are?

Exercise task 2

Who do you say you are? Being really honest, how would you answer using the core baseline 'I am' statements?

Often a key is to think what do you say about your 'self' when you make a mistake?

I am:

....

....

....

....

....

It is important to know that our minds are a battle field where many wars are won and lost over our self-evaluation and identity due to the influence of significant voices of others and the world. This war commenced from the moment we were conceived.

In the same way that a battle often rages in our minds and thought processes about the question of 'who am I,' it is clear that there was also a battle over Jesus' identity. As is the case for the majority of us, there were significantly positive voices and also those of a significantly negative influence that were spoken and heard throughout Jesus' life regarding his identity.

In the gospels we see his identity being affirmed by God and man:

God: "And a voice from heaven said, 'This is my beloved son, and I am fully pleased with him.'" *Matthew 3:17 (NLT)*

Man: Simon Peter answered "You are the Messiah, the son of the living God" *Matthew 16: 16 (NLT)*

We also see that Jesus recognised when his identity was significantly challenged; spiritual warfare took place over his identity that involved his adversary Satan, and men.

The statements began with *'If you are.'*

Satan: "*If you are* the Son of God, change these stones into loaves of bread." *Matthew 4:3 (NLT)*

Jews: "*If you are* the Messiah, tell us plainly." *John 10:24 (NLT)*

Chief Priests: "So he is the king of Israel, *is he*? Let him come down from the cross, and we will believe in him!" *Matthew 27:42 (NLT)*

Passer's by: "*If you are* the Son of God, save yourself" *Matthew 27:40 (NLT)*

Rulers: "Let him save himself *if he is* really God's chosen one, the Messiah." *Luke 23:35 (NLT)*

As Believers it is important to realise that Jesus understands what it is like to engage in the battle that takes place in our minds over the question of our identity: the 'who am I?' question.

Jesus was able to resist the arguments and pretentious '*if you are*' statements because of what he believed about his 'self' identity:

- He knew who had sent him.

- He knew his reason for being here.

- He knew who he was.

He knew who had sent him

"Don't you believe that I am in the Father and the Father is in me?" *John 14:10 (NLT)*

"I have come to you from God. I am not here on my own, but he sent me." *John 8:42 (NLT)*

He knew his reason for being here

"My purpose is to give life in all its fullness." *John 10:9 (NLT)*

He knew who he was

"*I am* the living bread that came down out of heaven."
John 6:51 (NLT)

"*I am* the light of the world." *John 8:12 (NLT)*

"Before Abraham was, *I am*." *John 8: 58 (NLT)*

"*I am* the gate. Those who come in through me will be
saved." *John 10:9 (NLT)*

"*I am* the good shepherd. The good shepherd lays down his
life for the sheep." *John 10:11 (NLT)*

"*I am* the Son of God." *John 10:36 (NLT)*

"*I am* the resurrection and the life." *John 11:25 (NLT)*

"*I am* the way the truth and the life. No one can come to the
Father except through me." *John 14:6 (NLT)*

"*I am* the true vine, and my Father is the gardener."
John 15:1 *(NLT)*

Jesus demonstrates by his core baseline '*I am*' statements that
He knew the answer to his 'who am I?' identity question.

Reflection Time

For some, considering personal genealogy, or as the Maori call it, 'whakapapa', is critical to 'self' identity, as defined by personal ancestry. Jesus' identity as a descendant of Abraham and David is outlined in the Gospel of Matthew.

Jesus' genealogy is as controversial as it may be for the reader in considering theirs; it includes Jacob, Judah, Tamar (who seduced Judah by posing as a prostitute), the Canaanite prostitute Rehab, Bathsheba (the focus of David's adultery and the reason for Uriah's murder) and the Kings whose failure led to the exile of Israel.

Jesus too has skeletons in his family closet! The important thing to remember is that as you consider your 'whakapapa' God is sovereign and can heal the consequences of our past.

Exercise task 3

As we have considered the battle for our minds, reflect on what it means for you personally that Jesus understands the 'mind battle' about self-evaluation.

....

....

....

....

....

Let us consider the three important points we have just discussed about Jesus' identity and how that may impact our identity as followers of Jesus:

Jesus	Followers of Jesus
He knew who had sent Him.	*We are a new creation.*
He knew His reason for being here.	*Our reason for being here.*
He knew who He was.	*Who are we?*

We are a new creation

"Therefore, if anyone is in Christ, he is a new creation; the old has gone, the new has come!" *2 Corinthians 5:17*

It is important to take a moment to recognise the implications of this truth. Because of the work that took place on the cross the truth is:

- We are complete in Christ, even though we may not feel complete.

- As we become Christians we become part of a new family; God is Father, and in Christ we are adopted into the family of God. *Ephesians 1:5*

Old creation	New creation
Old ways of thinking about oneself	Believing the truth of how God sees us
Separated from God	Adopted by God
In the world, subject to its systems	In the world but not of the world
Enemies of God: in our minds	Friends of God: renewed in our minds
Motivated by selfish interest	Under Grace, motivated by God's spirit
Getting our own way but never satisfied: Hostility, quarrelling, jealousy, anger, impure thoughts, sexual immorality	Living God's way: Love, joy, peace, patience, kindness, goodness, faithfulness, gentleness
Addictions	Self-control

Becoming a new creation radically affects our identity. We are made complete because of the cross; God has made a way for us through his Son. God's love is truly remarkable, dividing the old 'self' from the new 'self.' We are each on a journey of understanding what this truth means in relation to how we perceive 'self'. We are discovering who the true 'self' is!

Our reason for being here?

We were born to be image bearers, each of us are made in the image of God, in his likeness. We were born to have relationship with God and to make manifest God's Glory; we are heirs of God and co-heirs with Christ.

"That through the church the manifold wisdom of God might now be made known to the principalities and powers in heavenly places." *Ephesians 3:10*

The church is made up of individual believers and our role is to reflect the wisdom of God to all around us. We each have a significant identity in Christ, we are loved by him and our role is to reflect him to others.

Who are we?

We are adopted children of God.

Before becoming believers we lived our lives separated from God, we were the old creation. Like Adam we were separated and orphaned from God; we did not know God as our Father. We lived under the rules of Satan, the father of lies. Remember how Adam and Eve listened to Satan's voice and how they became separated from God. Ephesians 2:12 describes how we were without hope and without God in the world.

However, at the perfect time Father God sent his son into the world so that we could be delivered from Satan and his lies, we were far away but have been brought near through the blood of Jesus. We are now chosen and adopted as sons and daughters. This truth means we do not need to listen to any more lies from significant others regarding our identity. *Galatians 4:5 (Personalised)*

Adoption itself is a legal process, but God's adoption is more than a legal contract, this is a relationship of promise and we are made heirs; it is an unconditional gift. God's adoption is a permanent adoption. No matter your earthly background or status the truth about your identity is that you are loved and adopted into the family of God, you are unconditionally loved by Father God. You did not work for this adoption.

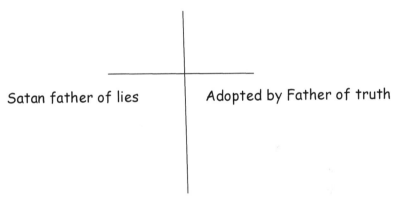

Satan father of lies   Adopted by Father of truth

Jesus made the way through

Because we are a new creation in Christ we have a whole new identity. When asked the question, 'who do you say that you are?' The truth filled answer is:

"I am a child of God, an heir." *Galatians 4:7 (Personalised)*

"I am adopted." *Ephesians 1:5 (Personalised)*

"I am loved. I cannot be separated from God's love." *Romans 8: 28 (Personalised)*

"I am complete in Christ." *Colossians 2:9-10 (Personalised)*

"I am God's workmanship." *Ephesians 2:10 (Personalised)*

Our identity is to be found 'in Christ', this is what it means to be complete. It is not based on 'feelings' but on the truth of our relationship with God. The truth of what He says about us. This is often where the battle takes place. Do we really believe these answers?

Reflection Time

For many of us the experience of early years has raised issue with our 'self' identity and the 'who am I?' question. Life from earliest memories may have included the absence of good things, perhaps failing to meet up to parental standards, involving mistreatment physically, emotionally, sexually, and for some spiritually. Many individuals will have experienced rejection, shame, betrayal and hurt in many and varied forms.

For others the wounding arrows of the negative significant voice and its message will have been more subtle; however the wounds will still have been present and will have challenged their sense of significance, security, and acceptance. Thus the core question regarding 'self' identity will have been asked.

As the saying goes: hurt people, hurt people. And so it goes on. Let us remember that Jesus suffered on the cross for our sin but also for the consequences of man's sin, which has blitzed and hurt the human race from one generation to the next.

Redemption took place in the body of Jesus. Jesus suffered because he bore in his body man's sin, and the consequences and hurts of sin down through all generations from Adam and Eve.

Jesus understands what it is to be hurt and wounded!

- Jesus was betrayed by his friends and left abandoned.

- Jesus suffered mental and emotional pain causing him to weep blood.

- Jesus suffered physical abuse, he was whipped and beaten.

- Jesus suffered emotional abuse, his identity was questioned. He was mocked and laughed at.

- Jesus was stripped naked and was crucified on a cross.

- Jesus was separated from his Father.

'Though he had done no violence, nor was any deceit in his mouth.'

Jesus took on himself our physical pain and sickness, and all our emotional pain. His blood cleanses all sin and its consequences: where we have been defiled and wounded by others He brings healing.

Matthew 26: 36 - Mark 14:32 - Isaiah 53; Jesus suffering on our behalf.

The more we recover the truth of our identity the more the five interconnecting areas of the 'self' will be influenced and restored. (Thoughts, emotional self, physical self, behaviours, our relationship with God) However we need to recognise and remember that just as Jesus' identity was challenged by Satan and man when he was on earth, so too there is a battle now being fought over each individual believer and the truth of their identity in Christ.

The model of 'self' becomes:

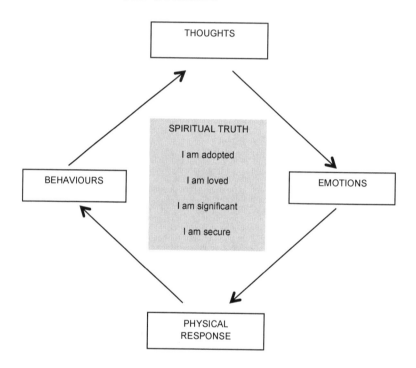

Satan does not want believers to walk in the truth of who they are, as a new creation with an identity in Christ; nor does he want Believers to be healed from the distorted self-image held from the past.

The strategic battle field for our identity takes place in the mind; how we think, the core baseline beliefs we hold about the 'self 'is the issue fought over. The battle rages between the truth of God's opinion about you and the lies voiced by Satan and significant others.

If we were to liken the mind to a computer, when it receives a virus the computer can display bizarre behaviour with loss of data. Similarly, our complex minds receive negative input about the 'self', which over time produces negative thoughts, these become negative core baseline beliefs that affect our sense of identity and ultimately our behaviour. Our imaginations can create either a work of art that is beautiful, or a horror movie. When we regularly focus on the negative, the critical and the judgmental perceptions about the 'self' we are living the horror movie, indeed we become self-prejudicial.

Samuel Smiles wrote:

'Sow a thought and you reap an act,

Sow an act and you reap a habit,

Sow a habit and you reap a character,

Sow a character and you reap a destiny!'

The thoughts we entertain play a significant role in increasing or decreasing emotional health and therefore self-esteem. It is a stark truth to realise that so many thoughts and actions in our life speaks of allegiance to God or to Satan.

The truth is:

- We are a new creation and we are to be made new in the attitude of our minds as we re-think our identity. *Ephesians 4: 22-24, Romans 12: 1 -2.*

- We are to demolish arguments and every pretension that sets itself up against the knowledge of God, about our true identity. To say of self: 'I am stupid,' 'I am no good', 'I am never going to amount to much'; is against and in disagreement with the way God sees you and what God says about you! *2 Corinthians 10:3-6*

- We are to take captive every thought to make it obedient to the truth of how God perceives us. *2 Corinthians 10:3-6*

- We are instructed to set our minds on the things above. *Colossians 3:2, Romans 8:5*

- We are not to conform any longer to the pattern of the world, but are to be transformed by the renewing of our minds; we are not to listen and agree with the negative significant voices of Satan, self or others.

The Recovery Curve diagram helps illustrate some of the steps to be taken in the process of restoring a distorted or damaged self-evaluation and later modules will focus on challenging our negative thoughts.

What does a healthy self-esteem look like?

So what does healthy self-esteem look like? It is evidenced when we believe and acknowledge that we are valuable, but no more valuable than those around us. A healthy self-esteem is to hold the core belief that we are of worth, significance, and are accepted and secure in Christ. From that place of security we are then able to give and receive love and find hope and fulfilment in relationships.

The ultimate source of a healthy self-esteem is found in relationship with the One who made us. It is not dependent on what we do or on a need to adapt our behaviours in order to earn love, significance or acceptance.

We are a new creation and are becoming whole persons as we come into in the presence of God, focusing on and listening to the words Father God speaks. It is in this place of relationship that the new 'self 'is no longer in bondage to the significant voices that the old 'self' listened to and believed.

In essence we move from separation from God to a place of reunion with God due to the resurrection work of Jesus on the cross: a renewing transformation takes place. The theologian Tom Wright explains that the risen Jesus is the first part of 'earth' to be transformed into a 'new creation', into which heaven and earth are joined. With the coming of the Holy Spirit, some of the creative power of God comes from heaven to earth to transform the bodies, minds, hearts and lives of the followers of Jesus. We too become a new creation.

"His transformed body is now the beginning of God's new creation ... heaven and earth will come together in a new way. Jesus' risen body is the beginning of that, the beginning of a heavenly reality which is fully at home on, and in, this physical world ('earth'), and the beginning of a transformed physical world which is fully at home in God's sphere ('heaven')". [6]

"Heaven and earth are joined together in Jesus; heaven and earth will one day be joined fully forever". [7]

See *Ephesians 1:10, Revelation 21:1-5*

Exercise task 4

Take a moment to ponder what it means for you to consider the truth that you are a new creation? (Believing the truth of how God sees you, adopted by God, living with a renewed mind).

....

....

....

....

....

---

[6] Acts for Everyone: Part 1 by Tom Wright: page 3

[7] Revelation for Everyone by Tom Wright: page 188

HOME ACTIVITY

- As you reflect on the 'Recovery Curve' diagram consider who you might go and talk to about your evaluation of 'self'.

- Consider how your self-evaluation has affected your relationships and your daily living activities.

- Reflect on how the significant voice/s of others has affected your self-perception.

- What does it mean for you to know that Jesus can identify with the battle that takes place in your mind regarding self-perception and evaluation?

- What are you going to take away and act on from Module 1?

Summary of module 1

ᕈ The model of 'self' includes the five personal interconnecting areas of the self that self-esteem affects. Each area is different and yet related: *Thoughts, emotions, physical response, behavioural response and the Spiritual self.*

ᕈ The Recovery Curve diagram helps to describe some of the steps to be taken on the journey of re-thinking the 'who am I?' question.

ᕈ The state of identity crisis commenced as God's enemy, our adversary Satan, tempted Adam and Eve to listen to a voice other than God's.

In the same way that a battle often rages in our minds and thought processes about the question of 'who am I', so too was Jesus' identity challenged and questioned.

The strategic battle field for our identity takes place in the mind; how we think, the core baseline beliefs we hold about the 'self' is the issue fought over.

A healthy self-esteem is to hold the core belief that we are of worth, of significance and are accepted and secure in Christ. From that place of security we are then able to give and receive love and find hope and fulfilment in relationships.

NOTES

His unchanging plan has always been to adopt us into his own family by bringing us to himself through Jesus Christ. And this gave him great pleasure.

Ephesians 1: 5 (NLT)

Module 2

What is Self-esteem?

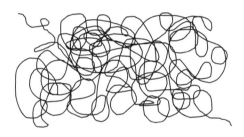

What a reassurance that at every stage of the journey through life, whether in the growing years of childhood, the demanding years of adult life and the significant years of retirement and ageing, God never wearies of us and never leaves us alone. [8]

---

[8] Colin Sinclair: Encounter with God: Scripture Union: July-Sept 2014

I am God's workmanship

Ephesians 2:10 (Adapted)

Introduction

As part of an integrative approach to understanding and answering the question of 'who am I?' the last module explored some of the biblical foundations of identity in order to have a truth base from which to move forward in the journey of recovery.

This module will now consider how negative beliefs about one's 'self' can develop from early childhood and as a consequence of later life experiences. It is important to understand the origins of how and why we come to think about 'self' the way we do and the impact of these beliefs on our daily living activities and relationships, with self, others and God.

Our earlier or later life experiences may include physical, psychological and spiritual wounding(s) that have led to the forming of negative core baseline beliefs. Sometimes the physical hurts are easier to name and more tangible than psychological or spiritual hurts and wounds. All wounds however will affect our sense of dignity, our self-worth and therefore self-identity.

It is important to give 'self' permission to tell our personal story and name our hurts with the consequential emotional pain; i.e. rejection, fear, shame. As we face the loss of what was or might have been, we may well experience a grief which in time may lead to anger at others, at ourselves, or indeed toward God for letting there be such hurt or cruelty in the world.

At times spiritual and psychological wounding seems harder to name or to take hold of than physical hurts because it is not always initially seen. However, physical, spiritual and psychological wounding does attack self-identity and our sense of self-worth as a human being. It attacks, indeed invades, our need for security, significance, and acceptance.

Desmond & Mpho Tutu ask the important question: "We can call out for help when someone is attacking us physically, but what aid do we need when the attack is emotional, when we feel ignored or rejected or slighted?" [9]

With each hurt or wounding there will be an impact on one's dignity, on one's sense of self-evaluation and worth as an individual. There will be a consequential formation of negative core baseline beliefs formed about our self-identity which in turn will affect our behaviours: these beliefs will impact the question of 'who am I?'

Understanding self-esteem

As people we have the ability to both be aware of ourselves, and also to place a value or measure of worth to ourselves or aspects of ourselves. We may use words like self-identity, self-image, self-perception, self-acceptance or we may use the words self-esteem. All refer to the opinions we have about

---

[9] The Book of Forgiving by Desmond & MphoTutu

ourselves, the judgments we make about ourselves and the value we place on ourselves as individual people.

'Self' in the Concise Oxford Dictionary is described as a person's own individuality, the essence that distinguishes oneself from another person. The same dictionary describes esteem as: to think favourably of, to regard as valuable, give respect to. [10]

Exercise task 1

Take a few minutes to write a short honest description of yourself and your value:

....
....
....
....
....

Now consider:

1. How did you describe yourself?
2. What value did you place on yourself or aspects of yourself?
3. Is that value positive, balanced, or negative?

....
....
....

---

[10] The Concise Oxford Dictionary. New Edition 1982

....
....

It is important to be realistic and recognise that at times the value we place on ourselves will dip or peak depending on how we feel at a given moment. As we take the journey of recovery in re-thinking our identity it is helpful to ask the question:

- Is how I am feeling in line with the truth of who I am in Christ and what God says about me? (Consider module 1)

- Whose significant voice(s) am I listening to, past or present?

Positive self-esteem

Because we are made in the image of God we are all of intrinsic worth. Each person is of worth and is deserving of mutual and self-respect.

In the Bible we learn that God's desire for each person is that we live with a positive self-evaluation. A positive self-esteem will be evidenced in the way an individual thinks, feels and behaves, implying acceptance, respect and a positive belief about oneself.

When accepting your 'self', you can live comfortably with your strengths and weaknesses without harsh self-criticism, and with the ability to honour both yourself and others. When you have positive belief in your 'self' you feel that you deserve good things and have confidence to pursue your goals and ambitions.

Positive self-esteem comes from within, it is based on your core baseline beliefs and nurtures resilience. It enables you to live life consistently despite external life challenges. It means that you know your core value as a person and that it is not dependent on what others think of you or what you do.

It is worth noting that becoming successful and/or being a high achiever, or being well liked does not confer positive self-esteem. Indeed, those who are achievers, those who are talented and well liked often surprisingly doubt their own core value and are sometimes unable to find joy in their abilities and successes. Positive self-esteem is rooted in how, 'I evaluate and think about me.'

Positive self-esteem at its core is based on the truth that the source of life is God. By seeking Him first, by discovering who you are 'In Christ' and letting Him meet your needs, your self-evaluation will be increasingly healthy. You will have an increased knowing of who you are and be more able to answer the question: 'who am I?'

Low self-esteem

Conversely to have low self-esteem is to have a negative appraisal of oneself, judging oneself unfavourably. People with low self-esteem have negative core baseline beliefs about the self; their thoughts are shaped by these beliefs and their rules for living are developed to protect themselves.

It is important to recognise that one's negative core baseline beliefs are often held as facts rather than opinions about the identity of 'self'.

CASE EXAMPLE - Chris

Chris was an office worker who had grown up with four younger siblings. His Father travelled much due to his occupation and when he was at home he was authoritarian in his disciple style and always tired.

This caused Chris to be fearful of his Father and he learned to be quiet in his Fathers presence so as not to displease him. Chris interpreted his Father's absence and his authoritarian approach as a failure on his behalf to be likeable, Chris developed core baseline beliefs: 'I'm a failure' and 'I'm not good enough.' Chris also developed an underlying fear of authority figures believing them to be severe and dominant.

As such core baseline beliefs about 'self' are held to be true: 'I'm a failure,' 'I'm not good enough', can have a negative impact on a person and this is reflected in the way they live out their daily lives.

For example when someone feels threatened in some way (emotionally or physically), they may experience negative or self-critical thoughts, which can alter mood and affect how they then behave.

CASE EXAMPLE - Chris

Chris is sat at his desk at work and the manager asks to see him after lunch, he immediately feels anxious with the thoughts, 'I have done something wrong, I am useless, I am so incompetent.' Chris wants to avoid his colleagues and is unable to concentrate.

Because of low self-esteem Chris does not stop to think that the talk with his manager may have a positive outcome! Instead his focus is upon his self-critical thought and self-judgments.

People with low self-esteem often think of themselves critically and often compare themselves to others from a negative bias.

Exercise task 2

Take a few minutes to write down your typical self-critical thoughts:

....
....
....
....
....

Origins of low self-esteem

There are many reasons that we come to hold the positive and negative baseline core beliefs we have about ourselves.

We have considered the origins of identity-crisis and the battle that can take place in the mind of each individual.

Let us consider how this combines with early life experiences that include the family, personal experience and observations of other people or society and media when growing up. These can have powerful influences on our thoughts and beliefs at a time when views about oneself, other people, the world, our future and who God is, are just developing. As we consider what these experiences may include, make a note of how they might have affected you personally:

Exercise task 3

What others did or said:

....
....
....
....
....

The significant voices of the past, perhaps including the media, that stand in contention to the truth of God's words of life to us as individuals:

....
....
....
....
....

The family or other narratives that were told about you:

....

....

....

....

....

What was observed and how others treated or responded to you:

....

....

....

....

....

Let us initially consider the childhood experiences that lead to the development of positive self-esteem or a healthy self-evaluation. This may include:

- Knowing God as a good Father: knowing we are accepted, secure, significant.

- Being listened to.

- Being praised.

- Being spoken to respectfully.

- Receiving hugs and attention.

- Experiencing success.

- Having trustworthy friends.

- A presence of good things.

Now consider childhood experiences that may have led to the development of low self-esteem; that is low self-evaluation. These may include:

- A distorted view of God as a Father.

- Not being listened to.

- Being harshly criticised, teased, ridiculed, or ignored.

- Being expected to be perfect most of the time.

- Experiencing failure.

- Experiencing abuse: emotional, physical, sexual, spiritual.

- Failing to meet parental standards.

- Failing to meet peer group standards.

- An absence of good things.

- Receiving, or taking responsibility for other people's stress or distress.

- Being the odd one out at home or school.

- Being an object of prejudice.

People with low self-esteem often have a distorted view of who God is and how he perceives them as an individual. Unfortunately, in some circumstances, the church as an institution has brought very mixed messages about who God is and how he acts. Some individuals have been significantly hurt from within the church and relate this harm to God himself. This can profoundly affect a person's identity and sense of 'self'.

People with low self-esteem have often received the message as a child or young person that failed experiences amount to a failure of the whole 'self'. This misconception can result in a profound sense of shame. Rather than saying 'I have made a mistake', shame says 'I am a mistake'; shame personalises.

Low self-esteem is a consequence of the original identity crisis described in Module 1, including early childhood experiences and additional life experiences that have shaped core baseline beliefs about the 'self'.

Difficult or distressing experiences throughout life will influence self-belief and negative thinking. Significant experiences may include specific incidents, traumas or times of general unhappiness or dissatisfaction with oneself which may build or strengthen a belief of being inferior to other people, useless, unattractive, ugly, un-loveable, or a failure. Furthermore, a crisis of faith as a result of a trauma, an accident, sickness or possible bereavement will often cause a deep questioning of who God is.

The sum of all these events can be low self-esteem:

ORIGINAL IDENTITY CRISIS

+

CHILDHOOD EXPERIENCES

+

LATER ADULT EXPERIENCES

=

LOW SELF ESTEEM

Exercise task 4

As you look at the list of childhood experiences that significantly influence the evaluation of 'self', review each statement and consider what childhood experiences influenced your self-esteem?

1..

2..

3..

4..

5..

6..

7..

8..

9...

10...

Exercise task 5

Consider and note down later adult life experiences or traumas that have significantly influenced your evaluation of 'self.' Include possible disappointment with God.

1...

2...

3...

4...

5...

The consequences of low self-esteem

Holding negative baseline core beliefs about oneself affects one's whole personhood. Let us take a moment to recall the *Model of Self*, discussed previously in Module 1.

Model of Self: Five interconnecting areas of 'self':

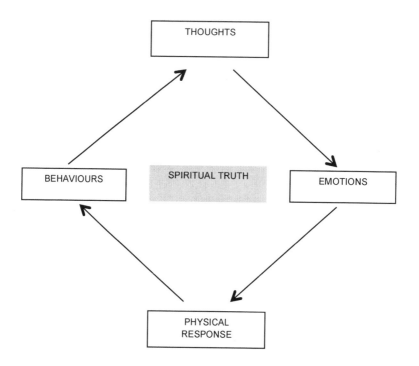

'Self' thoughts

Our thoughts can be healthy and produce a sense of well-being or they can be like a virus in a computer, creating havoc to our well-being.

In low self-esteem the thinking processes and thoughts about the 'self' are for a large part judgmental and self-critical, standing in opposition to God's spoken truth about an individual. The person's thoughts will be filled with self-doubt regarding their actions and abilities, and the individual will generally put 'self' down when things go wrong or when comparing to others.

Negative thinking processes can also serve to maintain a cycle of fear which helps maintain low self-esteem:

- There may be anticipatory anxiety when a person's thoughts focus on anticipating that things will not turn out well in a particular event, in turn maintaining a cycle of fear.

- A person's thoughts may tend to focus on past mistakes which maintains a cycle of self-criticism and self-doubt.

- When compliments are given the immediate thought is to brush them aside.

For example:

'I must be really stupid I didn't understand that lecture at all.'

'I'm so fat and useless.' (Often comparing self to someone else)

'Oh I've never done much with my life there is no point trying.'

'I'll never amount to much.'

'I will never be as good as …'

'I'm not going to go to the group, I probably won't fit in.'

'I worry that I will be different, will I find anyone who looks or speaks like me? Will I be accepted?'

It is worth remembering that a person's behavioural response to low self-evaluation thought processing can be on a spectrum from being quite withdrawn or avoidant, to over compensatory behaviour that may appear loud, pushy, or even comic, in order to mask their poor sense of self.

CASE EXAMPLE – Chris

When Chris was asked to see the manager his automatic thoughts were: 'I have done something wrong. I am useless. I am so incompetent.'

Chris started to anticipate what his manager may say to him. Because of an uneasy relationship with his Father and having had a harsh manager in the past, he anticipated all his mistakes would be highlighted.

Emotional self

It is important to recognise that negative self-critical thoughts effect our emotions and may cause low mood. The emotions experienced may be anxiety, depression, frustration, irritability, anger, guilt, shame, etc. As we learn to recognise when our mood / feelings alter it is helpful to begin to name the emotions.

CASE EXAMPLE – Chris

When Chris was asked to see his manager, rather than revert to being self-critical he could have asked himself:

- 'What does being asked to see the manager mean for me?'

- 'What emotions do I experience as a result of the request?'

It would then have helped Chris to have voiced them:

'When asked to see the manager...

I felt afraid

I felt anxious

I felt lonely

I felt ...'

Physical self

One's emotional state is often reflected in a physical response. An emotional response might be evidenced through an immediate discomfort in the stomach, a sense of panic, facial blushing or increased heart rate. There may be undue tiredness, low energy, alterations in posture with physical tension often in the neck and shoulders.

CASE EXAMPLE – Chris

As Chris sat waiting to see his manager he started to recognise that he felt weary, with tension in his neck and shoulders.

Behavioural responses

Because of the negative beliefs about the 'self' resulting in low mood and often physiological responses, our behaviour will be impacted. It is worth remembering that because someone is an apparent achiever or well liked, it does not automatically mean that the person has positive self-esteem.

Some behavioural consequences of low self-evaluation may be:

- Characteristic shyness or quietness, or always pushy and self-promoting.

- Facial expressions may alter with an avoidance of eye contact.

- Performance at work or college may alter. There may be a lack of motivation or over compensation resulting in working extra hard in order to look good.

- In relationships people may become upset by disapproval or they may seek to be people pleasers in order to receive praise which enhances self-worth.

- A person may avoid confrontations because they feel inadequate to deal with difficult situations. This may result in being bullied or abused.

- Others may avoid intimate relationships because they have no sense of worth.

- Sometimes self-care may be neglected or there may be an over compensation with a need to appear just perfect.

- When people do not value themselves they may drink excessive amounts of alcohol, abuse drugs or self-harm.

- Avoidance and the use of safety behaviours are often used to protect the individual's belief about their worth or value.

As individuals our behaviour and how we act will show what we believe about ourselves. Our sense of 'self-worth,' or what we believe about our 'self' will be reflected and evidenced in our behaviour, through our daily living activities and our relationships with self, others and God.

CASE EXAMPLE – Chris

When Chris was asked to see his manager he wanted to avoid his colleagues and was unable to concentrate on his work due to feeling fearful, anxious and lonely. He wanted to go and hide.

Relationship with God

For some the plea may be, 'God, help!' Often however when struggling with low self-worth our focus is usually on the critical 'self' and God's truth is no longer the centre of our thoughts or beliefs; though in reflective moments we may ask: 'God where are you?'. There may be an awareness of a sense of missing one's relationship with God, but not knowing how to find relationship with Him. Alternatively there may be an avoidance of God where the individual avoids taking time with him, choosing not to enter his presence.

The key to a healthy self-identity is to identify the battle in our mind and then in each circumstance to ask: 'whose significant voice is being listened to?' In any given moment there is a need to establish whether you are perceiving the negative voice of self or others, or the truth of who 'I am' in Christ.

Indeed we need to learn to discern between the voice of Satan our adversary which would push us back into the 'orphan' mentality; the significant voices of others that have been internalised from earlier childhood experiences, and repeated internal narratives told about 'self' from recent traumas?

For example: 'You are so thick'; 'you are always so clumsy'; 'you were never going to amount to much'; 'you were never good at making friends'; 'you were always hopeless at handling money, you will never change'.

Low self-evaluation causes an identity crisis when we surrender and agree to the negative bias of our thinking processes and believe the self-critical, self-judgmental thoughts about the 'self'. We are then no longer living with God at the centre of our lives but are surrendering to arguments that stand in opposition to the truth of what God says about an individual's worth.

CASE EXAMPLE – Chris

Chris had grown up going to church but had always seen God as an authoritarian figure who was not interested in him personally. It was only as an adult that he started to discover more of how God perceived him. He then began to realise that it was possible to have a personal relationship with God and that God deeply loved him and was not like his birth Father.

Consequences of low self-evaluation for Chris:

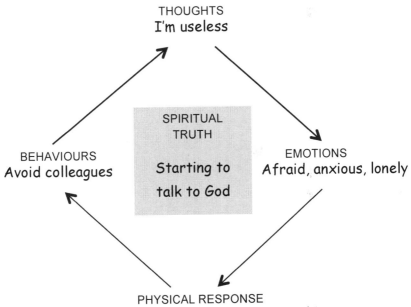

THOUGHTS
I'm useless

SPIRITUAL
TRUTH

Starting to
talk to God

BEHAVIOURS
Avoid colleagues

EMOTIONS
Afraid, anxious, lonely

PHYSICAL RESPONSE
Weary with tension in neck and shoulders

Low self- evaluation can be hidden behind many facades. We all at some stage of our life journey will battle with low self-confidence. Consider how low self- esteem may have affected you.

Exercise task 6

Thoughts about 'self'

....
....
....
....
....

Emotional responses

Make a note of the emotions you feel when battling low self-esteem:

....
....
....
....
....

Physical responses

Make a note of your physical responses when you experience low self-esteem:

....
....
....
....
....

Behavioural responses

Make a note of what you do or would like to do when experiencing low self-esteem: (Avoidance, withdrawing, being too pushy, use of safety behaviours)

....
....
....
....
....

Spiritual responses

How does your perception of God or your perception of 'self' in relation to God change when struggling with low self-esteem: (Avoiding, angry, longing for God?)

....
....
....
....
....

Exercise task 7

Having completed the above exercise have a go at mapping your own self-esteem chart.

Consequences of low self-evaluation:

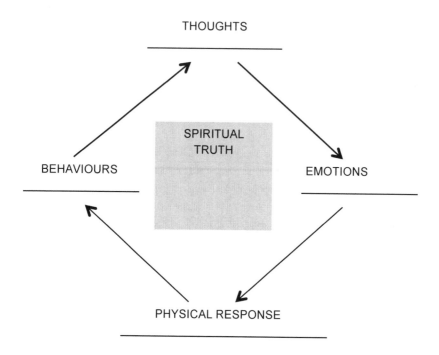

As we understand that self-esteem is about an individual's held core baseline beliefs and the consequential judgemental thoughts made about 'self', we start to realise the impact it has on the question of 'who am I?' Increased understanding of our 'self' judgements enables us to begin to comprehend and evaluate the impact a low self-evaluation can have on our concept of the 'self'.

The following diagram is adapted from a Cognitive Behavioural model of distress. It integrates a Biblical and psychological perspective.

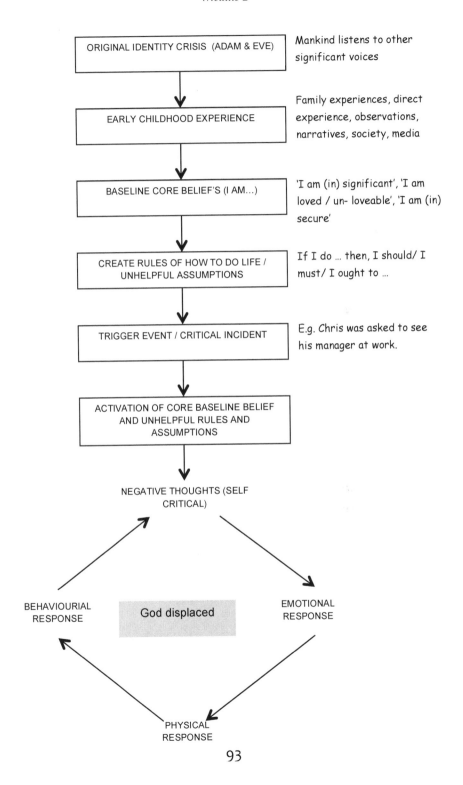

| ORIGINAL IDENTITY CRISIS (ADAM & EVE) | Mankind listens to other significant voices |

EARLY CHILDHOOD EXPERIENCE — Family experiences, direct experience, observations, narratives, society, media

BASELINE CORE BELIEF'S (I AM...) — 'I am (in) significant', 'I am loved / un- loveable', 'I am (in) secure'

CREATE RULES OF HOW TO DO LIFE / UNHELPFUL ASSUMPTIONS — If I do ... then, I should/ I must/ I ought to ...

TRIGGER EVENT / CRITICAL INCIDENT — E.g. Chris was asked to see his manager at work.

ACTIVATION OF CORE BASELINE BELIEF AND UNHELPFUL RULES AND ASSUMPTIONS

NEGATIVE THOUGHTS (SELF CRITICAL)

BEHAVIOURIAL RESPONSE

God displaced

EMOTIONAL RESPONSE

PHYSICAL RESPONSE

Exercise task 8

Childhood experiences and then later adult experiences significantly influence our concept of the 'self' and the judgments we go on to make about ourselves. These experiences help form core baseline belief statements which we hold as facts about who we are; they help form our core baseline 'I am' beliefs. As you review childhood experiences that have impacted your self–evaluation complete the following:

Family experiences in childhood:

....
....
....
....
....

Direct/ personal experiences:

....
....
....
....
....

Spiritual experiences when growing up:

....
....
....
....
....

Observations; things I saw happen to others:

....
....
....
....
....

Narratives; the repeated stories told about you:

....
....
....
....
....

Messages from society, culture, media:

....
....
....
....
....

Personal adult experiences:

....
....
....
....
....

What core baseline beliefs have you formed about yourself? What core baseline 'I am 'statements would you use to describe yourself?

I am:

....

....

I am:

....

....

I am:

....

....

I am:

....

....

CASE STUDY

Read the case study about Mrs. Oak and answer the questions below:

Mrs Oak

When I was growing up we had little money and my parents were in and out of work, we lived on a housing estate where unemployment was high. People like teachers, our GP, my parents' employers – they were people who appeared to have much more power in society than we did as a family. As I grew up I passed exams that enabled me to go to grammar school which meant my estate friends didn't want to hang out anymore. The problem was, I felt different from the other kids and felt unsure about bringing friends home to our estate. I guess I felt awkward and probably ashamed. I used to think we were different and they were better than us. As a child I used to go to Sunday school and came away feeling hopeful. Then I went away to University. Well, my Dad struggled with my leaving and then he disliked meeting 'those other people', as he would call them; he meant other parents. He never really came to see where I studied because he too felt different. I met other students who were interested in knowing God and I tried going to some of their groups.

Today those past experiences can sometimes affect how I feel in relation to people from more privileged backgrounds. I'm not always able to be spontaneous in their presence and I can need reassurance before I can trust that I will be accepted despite having become a teacher myself. I know academically I am able, I know God loves me but sometimes I just feel desperate to know more of Him. Sometimes I feel as though I'm out of my comfort zone when I'm with a lot of professionals.

For example, at a multi- disciplinary meeting for work I can just feel awkward. I think to myself, 'you will never be one of them.' Socially it sometimes feels like a huge leap into an unknown social world. I will often not go to things because I worry whether or not I will be accepted. If I do go I will feel stressed and will take a long time to consider what to wear. It is like my past has this invisible hold on me.

How would you rate Mrs. Oak's level of self-evaluation? (0 is low)

0	1	2	3	4	5	6	7	8	9	10

What are your reasons for this?

....
....
....
....
....

Can you identify her thoughts?

....
....
....
....
....

What emotions did she experience?

....
....
....
....
....

How was her behaviour affected?

....
....
....
....
....

Whose significant voice/s from the past may Mrs. Oak be listening to?

....
....
....

....

....

What aspects of her daily life can be problematic?

....

....

....

....

....

Where does God feature in Mrs. Oak's life experience?

....

....

....

....

....

Self-esteem questionnaire

For some people it is helpful to complete a questionnaire as a means of exploration, assessment or evaluation of low self-esteem.

The National Association for Self-esteem (NASE) offers a 'Self-Guided Tour' which helps you to gauge your level of self-esteem. It's called the Rosenberg's Self-Esteem Scale. [11]

The Rosenberg's Self-Esteem Scale is available online. The scale has the following 10 questions which you answer by rating yourself.

1. *I feel I am a person of worth, at least on an equal plane with others.*

2. *I feel I have a number of good qualities.*

3. *All in all, I am inclined to feel that I am a failure.*

4. *I am able to do things as well as most other people.*

5. *I feel I do not have much to be proud of.*

6. *I take a positive attitude toward myself.*

7. *On the whole I am satisfied with myself.*

8. *I wish I could have more respect for myself.*

9. *I certainly feel useless at times.*

10. *At times I think I am no good at all.*

---

[11] Rosenberg's Self-Esteem Scale: (NASE) National Association for Self Esteem: their 'Self-Guided Tour.'

HOME ACTIVITY

- Think about the development of your own self-esteem in relation to life experiences.

- What adult experiences have distorted your self-esteem?

- Think about what is keeping your low self-esteem going?

- What does it mean for you to be made in the God's image and to know the truth explained in Romans 8:38?

  "I am loved. I cannot be separated from God's love."

- Keep a journal and make a note of your 'Recovery Curve' journey.

- Have a look at the Rosenberg's Self-Esteem Scale easily available on line.

- What are you going to take away and what will you act on from Module 2?

Summary Module 2

 Self-esteem refers to how we view ourselves, and the value or measure of worth we place on ourselves or aspects of ourselves.

 Low self-esteem is having an overall negative opinion of oneself, judging or evaluating oneself negatively.

 Negative core beliefs about one's 'self' are often taken as facts, as the truth about one's 'self' rather than an opinion.

 Low self-esteem can have a negative impact on a person (self-criticism) and on their life style. (Self-care, relationships, work, leisure).

 We are all made in the image of God and are made to be his reflectors.

Because of Jesus dying on the cross all individuals can become a new creation in Christ. Each of us can leave the 'old' self behind.

The negative significant voices of the past no longer need to dominate our self-evaluation.

Our minds are a battle field where many wars are won and lost about over our identity.

It is important that we find a genuine sense of who we are in relation to God and his love for us. He is the source of our identity. In Christ we are fully known and loved and through Him we can know true completeness.

NOTES

I am loved. I cannot be separated from God's love.

Romans 8:39 (Adapted)

Module 3

What Maintains Low Self-esteem?

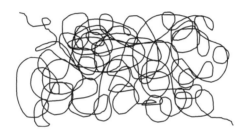

It is very important to know that the true self is not moral perfection or even psychological wholeness. Many masochistic saints, eccentric prophets, and neurotic mystics are more than a bit strange, and they almost always have serious blind spots, but they knew who they were in God and knew how to return there. That is their secret. [12]

---

[12] Immortal Diamond by Richard Rohr: Page 51

I am a child of God, an heir.

Galatians 4:7 (Adapted)

Introduction

Module 2 considered how negative beliefs about one's 'self' can develop from childhood and as a consequence, of later life experiences. The module explored the importance of understanding the origins of how we think about 'self', the reasons we think this way, and the impact of these beliefs on our daily living activities and relationships with self, others and God.

Module 3 will now explore how negative beliefs about the 'self' are maintained. As part of understanding low self-esteem it is important to understand why negative beliefs about ourselves can persist long after the experiences involved in their formation have passed. This module will talk about how and why negative beliefs about the self are maintained.

How negative beliefs about the 'self' are maintained

Our negative self-beliefs have most of their origin in our early life experiences. Because there is so much constantly happening in the world around us, our brain has to choose what to pay attention to, how to process our thoughts and how to make sense of all the information. Often what we *pay attention to* and how we think about these things, or *our interpretation*, form the beliefs we hold about 'self'.

We interpret events as a child or adolescent and from these appraisals we form conclusions about our 'self.' Some will be positive judgments, others will be self-critical judgments. Often as adults the things we do on a daily basis keep the negative self-critical judgments we formed about ourselves in our early experiences active and alive.

As adults we interpret the information from the world around us through the lens of the unhelpful judgments, assumptions and rules we formed in the past. This process helps maintain the negative core baseline beliefs about ourselves; rather like wearing old spectacles fitted with old lenses which distort vision in the here and now.

CASE EXAMPLE - Chris

Remember Chris? He was appraising the 'here and now', being called to his manager's office, through the old lens of his negative early childhood experience of a domineering authoritarian adult figure.

Our thoughts become a personal internal commentary on life. Negative thoughts therefore play a vital role in maintaining low self-esteem. We all talk to ourselves; 'self-talk' makes up a large percentage of our thinking and if our self-talk is too negative it can result in significant loss of confidence. It is therefore important to recognise and understand the content of our personal self-talk and how it has been influenced by significant others in our lives. Unhelpful self-talk can focus inappropriately on how we perceive ourselves in relation to others.

The content of self-talk can be rejection focused; self-rejecting with self-criticism and self-judgments, for instance: 'they will think I'm stupid', 'I'll never be as good as ...'

We have established that negative baseline core belief 'I am' statements, formed in early experiences (e.g. 'I am incompetent,' 'I'm not good enough'), influence our thoughts and behaviours as we become adults. In addition to these 'I am' statements we also pay attention to, and look out for, negative events that may confirm the original ideas formed about the 'self', with the result that over time we develop 'biased thinking.'

Biased thinking

The psychologist Melanie Fennell refers to 'biases in thinking', suggesting that there are two biases in thinking that maintain the negative beliefs about the self: biased self-perception and biased interpretation

Biased self-perception - A bias in how you see yourself.

When your self-esteem is low you will be quick to notice anything that is consistent with your low self-esteem and confirms the negative view you hold about yourself. This may relate to your appearance, your character, or behaviour. You will notice the ways that you do not come up to your ideal standard.

Low self-esteem can present itself as a fear of failure because of the internal striving perfectionist. A person with low self-esteem places the 'self' in a position of failure if standards are so high as to be unattainable, rather like someone setting the bar on the high jump at a height that just cannot be jumped; this can increase loss of confidence and cause anxiety. Equally many people ignore the positive aspects of 'self' which contradict the negative views of 'self', e.g. all qualities and strengths are reduced to the insignificant or quickly forgotten or dismissed.

Our biased self-perception is influenced by our internal thought commentary. It is important to consider whose voice of standards or rules we are living up to:

- Our own self-critical voice of self-talk.

- The significant negative voice of others.

- Your adversary the devil who opposes the truth and wants to keep everyone entrapped in an orphan mentality that says: 'you are stupid, ridiculous, not good enough, un-loveable or unlikeable, a failure, you don't belong.'

- The truth of what God says about you.

Perhaps it is necessary to ask the question; do we judge or evaluate others as harshly as we might judge or evaluate one's 'self'? So often we become our own personal taskmaster.

Biased interpretation - *The meanings attached to an event.*

As low self-esteem distorts the perception we hold of ourselves as a result of negative core baseline 'I am' statements, it also distorts the meanings we attach to an event.

For example if an event does not go well, someone with low self-evaluation may use this as the basis for a judgment of 'self'; it becomes personal. A small mistake may become a reflection of our worth. Rather than thinking, 'I have made a mistake', our judgment becomes personalised: 'I'm stupid', 'what an idiot'.

When our thinking is biased toward self-criticism we may be quick to dismiss praise when in fact others have noticed something positive about an event that went well.

Our negative beliefs are maintained over time because of what we *pay attention to* and how we *interpret* the incoming information.

Exercise task 1

Biased self-perception: A bias in how you see yourself.

Considering your own internal commentator, whose internal voice of standards or rules are you trying to live up to:

- Your own internal voice.

- The internal voice of significant others (i.e. the parental voice, teachers).
- Your adversary the devil.
- The truth of what God says about you.

Whose commentary are you listening to?

....
....
....
....
....

In bringing a sense of hope, whose voice is:

Helpful	Unhelpful
....	....
....	....
....	....
....	....
....	....

Do you ignore positive aspects of yourself?

(E.g. are your qualities and strengths ignored or dismissed?)

....
....
....
....
....

Write down some of your qualities and strengths.

....

....

....

....

....

....

It is important as individuals to choose the commentary that encourages and helps maintain a balanced view of your life and that speaks positively into your identity.

Exercise task 2

Biased interpretation: The meaning attached to an event or circumstance.

Re-consider a recent circumstance or event that you viewed negatively. What positives did you dismiss or ignore?

(If it helps, imagine asking a friend who also viewed the circumstance: what would their unbiased assessment of you have been?)

....

....

....

....

....

It is worth noting that as we reflect on some of our childhood events, biased interpretations will be discovered that will have negatively influenced the appraisal of 'self' in the here and now.

Low self-evaluation is influenced by *biased self-perception* and *biased interpretation* which serve to maintain low self-evaluation. Low self-belief is further maintained by the development of *biases in memory* and in *thinking*.

Biased memories

From our interpretation of events or our told narrative as a child or adolescent, we form conclusions about our core 'self' and others. This in turn will affect the memories we then hold. It is important to remember that our memories are a result of our interpretation of an event or our told narrative. That is why each person attending an event will have differing memories of it. Our memories hold our opinions, interpretations and judgments of an event. These memories can be distorted by our biased self- perceptions and biased interpretations.

Biased thinking styles

We are all prone at times to have negative thinking styles. Our style of thinking influences our emotions and behavioural responses. When we are tired, under stress or anxious, these styles may be more pronounced.

Disqualifying the positives: One rejects positive experiences. This can maintain a negative believe that is contradicted by everyday experiences.

Scanning: There is an increased awareness of anything that is consistent with our negative 'self' view.

Magnification or minimisation: One exaggerates the importance of things such as one's mistakes or someone else's achievements and/or inappropriately shrinks things. E.g. 'Brenda is an amazing Mum and is so creative; I'm just not creative and I'm a useless Mum.'

Over-generalising: Interpreting an event so that small mistakes are seen as a problem and a reflection of our worth as a person.

Personalising: You take the responsibility or the blame for anything unpleasant even when it has little or nothing to do with you: 'It's my fault.'

Catastrophising: One anticipates disaster as the only outcome, without considering possible alternatives.

Exaggerating: This involves an over-estimation of the chances of something negative happening or how bad it will be if the experience does happen.

All or nothing thinking: Seeing everything in 'black or white' thinking. There is little consideration of grey!

Jumping to conclusions: One makes a negative interpretation even when there are no definite facts.

Mind reading: You conclude that someone is reacting negatively to you, without evidence to support this.

Fortune teller: One anticipates that things will not go well and are convinced that their prediction is already an established fact.

Emotional reasoning: Believing that what you feel must be true – I feel a failure, therefore I am a failure. I feel hopeless, therefore I am hopeless.

Biases in thinking can cause disappointment in 'self' and toward others. This in turn serves to confirm negative beliefs and maintains the cycle of negative thinking that maintains low self-esteem.

Exercise task 3

When completing this task remember that the negative beliefs held about 'self' are opinions formed about identity rather than facts.

Consider the biased thinking styles and reflect on a recent circumstance or event when your estimation of yourself was low.

What was the event?

....

What was your emotional response?

....

What biased thinking styles did you use?

....
....
....
....
....

Prejudicial judgments

Our minds are a battle field where many wars are won and lost over our identity. It is important then to understand the deep impact of the commentary that takes place in our minds. It is necessary to consider whether that commentary is helpful or unhelpful. Does it match up with the truth of how God perceives you?

Christine Padesky, a Cognitive therapist suggests that the negative beliefs about the 'self' are similar to prejudices. The Concise Oxford dictionary describes 'prejudicial' as: 'causing prejudice'; when we are prejudicial against the 'self' we are causing prejudice and thereby harming the 'self'. A prejudice is a belief which does not take account of all the facts but relies on biased evidence for its support (as in biased self-perception and biased interpretation of events).

If negative core baseline beliefs become judgments against the 'self', we place 'self' in the role of Judge, as in a court. By doing this we make judgments and form opinions about the estimation of 'self' that are detrimental to the interests of our own identity. We become self-prejudicial by forming opinions about the 'self' without taking into account all the facts. In so doing we often ignore the 'evidence' that is contrary to the original low self-belief. We also ignore and discount the truth of what God says about us.

Imagine as an adult having an old school report from childhood that holds the commentary of many negative voices from the past, and still living under its effects: 'Should have tried harder,' 'Will never amount to anything,' 'Lacks confidence.' The report can feed the negative/low self-belief statements: 'I am hopeless' or, 'I'm never going to have enough of what it takes to make a difference.'

An individual could spend time looking for all the evidence to prove that the old report is still true by looking for biased evidence in daily living activities that confirm the written evidence in the report. In doing so, they would become self-prejudicial by ignoring important evidence to the contrary. By dismissing or ignoring the positive qualities and strengths about the 'self', the individual would maintain the low self-belief status.

Consider then having a new written report; it would be like a new beginning! Start to imagine what you would like to believe about your 'self' with no self- judgments and no old negative internal commentaries.

The report would especially take into account what God believes about you and would be an opportunity to renew your thinking about the identity of your 'self'. Reading an up-to-date report would create time to review and consider the evidence of God's perception of you, to reflect on his affirming words about you and look at true evidence that would influence your core baseline 'I am' statements. The new report would take into account all the positive qualities that have until now been ignored; you would indeed be re-thinking your identity.

The truth is, we cannot change the past and we don't know the future, but we can change the way we think about 'self'; this is called 'renewing the mind'.

Exercise task 4

Consider for a moment how your thoughts are prejudicial against your 'self': Write down some of your 'self' negative beliefs: note whether these are helpful (H) or unhelpful (U).

For example:

I'm just so rubbish, I have never been good at making friends. (U)

I'm not good at maths but that does not mean I am a failure. (H)

.... ( )

.... ( )

.... ( )

CASE EXAMPLE – Chris

Chris sat anxiously waiting to see his manager, all the while the battle in his mind was raging: 'You are so incompetent, you will have messed up.' Chris dismissed his recent excellent competency report. The more he focused on his self-prejudicial thoughts the more anxious and fearful he became.

Protecting our 'self': rules for living

As a result of earlier childhood experiences and possible negative life experiences we form negative beliefs about ourselves which we may not be aware of because they become so automatic.

For example, I was attending a course and was in a queue for a cup of tea. A lady before me made a mistake as she made her refreshment and her immediate audible verbal response to herself was 'I am so stupid.' It was just automatic!

Her negative core baseline beliefs might have been:

'I am not good enough'

'I'm unlovable'

'I'm a loser'

As we grow up, in addition to the formation of negative beliefs to enable self-survival, we begin to develop rules and guidelines about how to live our lives. These rules are created to help protect our sense of 'self' from our own painful, negative core baseline 'I am' beliefs (see model of low self-esteem diagram: Module 1). These rules become like an invisible wall around us or like an invisible container in which we unwittingly place our 'self'.

Rules for living and assumptions can come in the form of statements that are created as additional survival rules. These may include:

- I must do

- I should do

- I ought to do

For example:

'I must not show emotions'

'I must never make mistakes'

'I should always do my best'

We might also develop conditional assumptions:

- 'If I do ... then ...'

For example:

'If I let people really know me, they will not like me.'

'If someone does not understand me it is because I am unworthy of interest.'

'If I get high scores in my exams then I will be approved of.'

'If I adapt my behaviour then I will belong.'

'If I don't try anything then I won't fail and I won't be disappointed or disappoint others.'

In time rules and assumptions can be combined:

'I must always watch what I eat and stay slim then I will be accepted and loved.'

These assumptions and rules for living can bring:

- A conditional sense of worth and acceptance to our sense of 'self'.

- They can help us to function on a day to day basis.

- They enable us to feel comfortable with our 'self' as long as we can obey them.

- These rules help protect our low self-evaluation.

In the long term the rules for living and assumptions we create to protect our 'self' will affect our behaviours, our daily living activities and relationships. These rules take the form of coping strategies which detract from our relationship with God.

For example:

- The rule for living: *'I must always do well at work'* may protect against the negative baseline belief 'I'm a loser'; this will make the individual very careful about work, ensuring there are no mistakes. The rule assumes the negative core baseline is true and that it is indeed a fact. Although in the short term it acts as a protector, in the long term it maintains low self-evaluation.

- The rule for living: *'I must always watch what I eat and stay slim, then I will be accepted and loved'*, may protect the individual against the negative core baseline belief *'I'm unlovable.'* This assumption would influence behaviours by encouraging over-vigilance regarding food intake and content. Again the rule for living assumes the negative core baseline belief to be true!

Some of the consequences of rules for living and assumptions:

- Rules for living and assumptions prevent you from exploring whether your core baseline belief is true. These rules prevent you from disconfirming the core baseline beliefs.

- You can feel good about your 'self' only if the rules are fulfilled. For example, if you can always do well at work, or if you stay slim.

- You can become exhausted by the effort required to maintain the rules and assumptions for daily living.

- The rules are in place initially to protect one's sense of 'self', to defend 'self', to prove it or even to assert 'self'. However, it often means you do not get to know your 'true self' because of the fear of letting down the facades.

- The negative core baseline beliefs are still there but are hidden.

Richard Rohr explains that as people, we want constants and insurance policies at every stage of life. "But we have to be careful, or they totally take over (the rules) and become all controlling needs, keeping us from further growth."[13]

The rules that once were created to protect us become our 'keeper'. They keep us 'hooked in' and 'held captive' to the fear of 'what if'; if our rules fail us we will be faced with our painful core baseline beliefs.

Exercise task 5

What rules for living (I should, I must, and I ought to) and assumptions (if I do ... then ...) have you used to help you feel better about your 'self'?

....

....

....

....

....

---

[13] Falling Upward by Richard Rohr: Chapter 1: page 8

The useful function of low self—esteem

As we begin to recognise that *rules for living* and *assumptions* are initially put in place to protect against negative core baseline 'I am' beliefs it may be a surprise but also important to acknowledge that maintaining low self-evaluation can have possible benefits!

CASE EXAMPLE – Amanda

Amanda was an only child of older parents. She had gained a good degree and had always been expected to 'go far.' Amanda was 40 years old, had married, was recently divorced with no children, and was employed as a Personal Secretary.

Amanda believed she was a failure because she had been expected to 'go far'. Her parents had disapproved of her marriage believing her husband to be 'not good enough.' Amanda was convinced she had not achieved what her parents had expected of her. Some of Amanda's core baseline beliefs were:

'I am a failure'; 'I am not good enough.'

Amanda attended counselling and as we explored her possible conditional assumptions and rules for living, Amanda realised that one of her rules was:

'If I don't try to succeed then I won't fail.'

Amanda had used avoidance behaviours to protect her 'self' against her core baseline belief 'I am a failure', this in turn maintained her low self-esteem. The benefit of her low self-esteem was to protect

---

her from taking risks, from disappointment and from fear of failing. The consequence was that she would never prove to herself that she was capable of further success or achieve her desired potential. This resulted in her being frustrated and angry with herself. Amanda was living behind invisible walls.

CASE EXAMPLE – Luke

Luke was a successful Company Director, with a struggling marriage and successful older children who had left home. Luke had been fostered as a child and then adopted. He had always struggled with relationships, describing himself as 'a loner' (core baseline belief). Luke looked back over his life and realised he had colleagues but no real friends. He described himself as, 'I am an achiever' but, 'I am also empty' (core baseline beliefs).

As we explored why he had worked so very hard he realised that for him, work protected him from having to make relationships and yet 'if I work hard and succeed people will affirm me and then I feel good about myself' (assumption). He stated that, 'the problem is that when I am working I have a sense of wellbeing but when I am alone and not working I don't have a sense of being.'

Luke had no sense of 'being'; of knowing who he was. As he approached retirement he acknowledged that he blamed his low self-esteem on his past, his birth and adoptive parents. His past had caused him to protect himself by using 'rules for living.' These rules prevented him taking the risk of getting close to people and it enabled him to avoid responsibility for his behaviours.

The benefit of his low self-esteem was that he could avoid his anticipatory anxiety about being rejected by people; 'if I get close to people and they discover who I am they will not like me.' Luke's life was fear based, he was afraid of rejection with his core baseline belief being, 'I am un-loveable.' For Luke, working hard had resulted in him becoming a workaholic, but he was in control with the resulting benefit of affirmation and achievement.

Low self-esteem may benefit us by seeming to provide protection and safety for us, it may act as a defense for us, as a shield or refuge against our worst fears, that our core baseline 'I am' statements may be true. So we build false containers, or cisterns to protect 'self'.

By identifying the benefits (advantages), and costs (disadvantages) regarding the status of low self-evaluation we will start to see some of the challenges we face in improving our self-esteem and renewing our minds, indeed in 're-thinking identity: who am I?'

CASE EXAMPLE – Julie

Julie had grown up in difficult circumstances that resulted in her identifying her rule for living as, 'if I look after my-self then I will be alright.' Julie described herself as 'I am Miss Self-reliant.' (Core baseline belief)

With more exploration Julie realised that her rule for living and her core baseline belief about herself was in part maintaining her low self-esteem. Julie looked at the benefits (advantages), and costs (disadvantages) of her thinking processes:

'If I look after myself then I will be alright.'

'I am Miss Self-reliant.'

Benefits (advantages):

- Miss Self-reliant has given me a sense of control.

- Miss Self-reliant has given me some freedom.

- Miss Self-reliant gives me a confidence in my own achievements.

- Miss Self-reliant protects me from others.

- Miss Self-reliant gives me the power.

Costs (disadvantages):

- I feel lonely and unsupported.

- People presume I am ok and I'm not ok. Inside I'm really afraid and vulnerable.

- I am isolated and people don't know me.

- My world view is very individualistic and leaves me separate from others.

- I have not learned to trust others.

- Being Miss Self-reliant leaves God out of the equation.

As a result of looking at some of the benefits of maintaining low self-evaluation, versus the costs Julie was able to make a choice for her 'self'.

Did she want to face the challenges of changing her rules for living?

By identifying her rules Julie was commencing the process of renewing her mind, she was able to consider what this would mean for her sense of 'self' and how those changes in thinking would then impact her behaviours.

By identifying the benefits of low self-esteem we are able to see the challenge that we may have in improving our self-esteem.

For Julie it meant that she made choices about who she would begin to be more real and vulnerable with; she recognised her need to learn to trust others with her 'self.' Julie made decisions about taking risks in asking for help. Julie was surprised to realise her self-reliance had left God out of the 'equation of her life' and so she made decisions in relation to her relationship with God.

As we consider letting go of some of our rules for living let us ponder:

"God's own rules do not matter as much as the relationship that God wants to create with us... The genius of the biblical revelation is that it refuses to deny the dark side of things, but forgives failure and integrates falling to achieve it's only promised wholeness."[14]

---

[14] Falling Upward by Richard Rohr: The tragic sense of life: page 57

Exercise task 6

Consider some of the benefits of low self-evaluation

E.g: Benefit: Avoid failure ; Cost: Never prove I can suceed

Benefits	Costs
....	....
....	....
....	....
....	....
....	....

Exercise task 7

Identify some of the challenges you personally would face in your life in choosing to identify and re-think your evaluation of your 'self.' (Perhaps review Julie's benefit / cost analysis)

....
....
....
....
....

The problem with negative rules for living and assumptions is that it is assumed that they are true, indeed fact. One never gets the chance to put the negative core baseline beliefs to the test. They maintain negative thoughts about the 'self', ultimately restricting behaviours and standing in argument to the truth of how God perceives us.

CASE EXAMPLE – Luke and Julie

Luke never allowed himself to get close enough to others to be able to test and see if they would reject him. His rules for living and assumptions caused him to live in ways that were unhelpful. They prevented him from facing what he feared. This self-protective behaviour restricted him from living in ways that would allow him to have experiences that would enable him to identify and challenge his core baseline beliefs.

As Julie discovered, the rules for living may also significantly limit our relationship with God.

Avoidant and Safety Behaviours

Life is full of daily challenges to our self-evaluation. Each day we are faced with challenges that test our negative core baseline beliefs, rules for living and assumptions. There may be a real risk of not living up to our rules or avoiding our assumptions.

For example the rule 'I must never make mistakes' is unrealistic and hard to continually sustain. The result of this is that we become anxious and make anxious predictions. These predictions, what we think may happen, lead us to avoid situations, or to engage in behaviours that make us feel safe. Our rules will always be at risk of being broken so we take precautions.

Avoidance

Avoidance means not doing something because to do it would cause anxiety. We avoid or withdraw from situations due to fear and so participate less in everyday living activities. Avoidance will often make us very adaptive in our behaviour. We may become like Chameleons, always adapting in order to avoid painful emotions or what we perceive as difficult circumstances or events. This can lead to passive behaviour/s. Some individuals may avoid making decisions and always seek to please people because of the fear of rejection, being unacceptable, insignificant, or not belonging.

Avoidance makes sense from the self-protection point of view.

In the short term it may be one way of reducing anticipated anxiety or fear of the worst happening. However in the long term avoidance maintains low self-esteem because the fear behind anticipatory anxiety, what we fear may happen, is never disconfirmed. Over time this affects life style and relationships.

CASE EXAMPLE – Alisha

Alisha, a qualified health practitioner, had decided to stay at home to look after her children. Alisha described herself as lacking in confidence: 'I'm always worrying that I will make a mistake.' At times she wondered if she had made the decision to be at home because she so often felt anxious about what would be expected of her if she returned to work.

Each school day Alisha would take her girls to and from the school playground, always being careful to stand at the edge so the she wouldn't have to talk to lots of the other mothers. As the end of term drew near her youngest daughter wanted to give her teacher a gift.

On the last day of term in the afternoon Alisha went to collect her girls and as she was about to leave the teacher came into the playground. Alisha gave her youngest daughter the gift and told her to run and give it to the teacher. Alisha immediately quickly started to head towards the gate because she was fearful that the teacher may want to engage her in conversation, 'I would have been so embarrassed and would not have known what to say.' So Alisha just waved and walked away quickly in order to avoid a conversation. Afterwards Alisha felt ashamed and angry and thought how "stupid" she was.

Alisha's fear prevented her from talking to the teacher. She anticipated that she would be embarrassed and say the wrong thing. This led to avoidant behaviour, fleeing the conversation and included the use of safety behaviors: taking flight and leaving her daughter to give the present. This in turn reinforced Alisha's already low evaluation of her 'self' with the added introduction of self-critical and judgmental thoughts.

Safety Behaviours

These are behaviors that are used to help get through the situation that is causing anticipatory anxiety and helps to maintain a low self-evaluation. The motive is to protect 'self' when we fear the worst may happen.

Safety behaviours appear to make the situation easier but in fact makes them more difficult because they maintain our fears. Safety behaviours are unnecessary precautions and they never allow us to disconfirm the fears behind the behaviours, thus maintaining a sense of low self-evaluation.

Avoidance and safety behaviours for people with low self-esteem or a poor sense of 'self' can result in self-critical thinking and reduced self confidence.

The key is to face the fears without the use of precautions in order to discover if the fear has any reality. Anticipatory precautions suggest 'If I don't do ... then something will happen to me,' it is based on *biased thinking*.

Examples of safety behaviours:

- Agreeing with others rather than voicing what you really think.

- Talking to safe people about safe topics as you attend social events.

- Rehearsing conversations.

- Speaking very slowly or quietly, or too fast.

- Leaving the room immediately after a meeting in order to avoid conversations.

- Becoming the joker or never risking telling a joke.

- Not talking about yourself or your feelings.

- Passing a compliment off or putting 'self' down when a compliment is given.

- Waiting for someone else to arrive before entering a room of people.

Exercise task 8

As you consider your use of avoidant and safety behaviours it is helpful to review whether you were:

Overestimating the chance of the worst happening.

Overestimating how difficult it might be.

Underestimating personal strengths, skills, and abilities to handle the situation.

Underestimating the support of others.

Write down a situation that recently made you anxious:

....

....

....

....

....

What did you anticipate would happen? (Your worst fear)

....

....

....

....

....

What did you do to stop this happening? (Avoidance / Safety behaviours)

....

....

....

....

....

How did this affect your low self-esteem?

A - What thoughts / images did you have about your 'self'?

....

....

....

....

....

B- How did you feel emotionally?

....

....

....

....

....

How did using these self-protective behaviours (avoidance / safety behaviours) hinder your trust in God?

....
....
....
....
....

Start to pray about the fear behind why you avoid situations and why you use safety behaviours.

....
....
....
....
....

What could you do differently in the same situation next time?

....
....
....
....
....

The reality is that we all battle in our minds and all are on a journey of discovering our true 'self' identity. The use of avoidance and safety behaviours for people with low self-evaluation can result in self-critical thinking, reduced self-confidence and increased self-condemnation. Additionally rules of 'you should' have or 'you ought' to have done ... , are activated which can leave the person with a sense of increased inadequacy.

Reflection Time

Let us remember that the restoration of 'self' is found in relationship with God, in whose image we are made. Our sense of well-being develops as we discover more about our self-identity: 'who I am' in relationship with, and in the presence of God.

As a result of being in God's presence we can exchange every negative word from the world, every internal negative mind commentary, and / or every lie of Satan with the words of truth and abundant life that God is always speaking to us.

"I am loved. I cannot be separated from God's love." Romans 8:39.

- Security – 'I am secure'

- Acceptance – 'I am accepted'

- Significance – 'I am significant'

As the question of identity is being unravelled and we explore self-evaluation, it becomes apparent that dependency on inaccurate and biased thinking is often a reality. This inaccuracy always negatively shapes self-evaluation. Inaccuracy of thinking affects behaviours, emotional needs and indeed one's relationship with God. One's *sense of being becomes distorted.*

No one has a perfect upbringing and most will have received security, acceptance and significance to a measure. However words and life experiences will have impacted those levels and caused us to look for a 'top-up' of security, acceptance and significance from other sources, often from sources, people and places other than God. Metaphorically we often travel to distant lands like the Prodigal Son! Each of these man-made sources will in themselves be limited.

A genuine *sense of being* is primarily to be found in relation to God and in his presence. Only in him is the source of our identity found. This makes sense as we consider that we are made in the image of God. We were made to be in relationship with a loving Father who at the right time made a way for us to be adopted through his son. We are no longer orphans but are brought into the family of God.

It is important to involve God in the rebuilding of self-esteem, asking him to help us renew the distorted thinking of the mind. Ask him to help you gain a new picture of truth about your 'self'. Low self-esteem has fear at its root; a fear of being insecure (not belonging); a fear of being un-loveable (rejected); a fear of being insignificant (worthless).

Exercise task 8

Start to ask God to show you how the root of fear/s got access to your life.

Key questions may be:

When did I start to feel negative about my 'self' or become self-critical: Was it an early life experience, or the repeated told narrative, or a later life trauma?

(This will give an indication of what was happening at the time and what you were fearful of.
Remember it may be an absence of a good thing.
I.e. lack of affirmation).

....

....

....

....

....

What were the circumstances?

....

....

....

....

....

Who were the significant others involved? Whose voice(s) have been influential or absent in how I evaluate my 'self'?

....

....

....

....

....

Have there been significant incidents or difficult life experiences as an adult?

....

....

....

....

....

Have I maintained my low self-evaluation by my agreement with inaccurate and biased thinking about myself?

....

....

....

....

....

As you consider these questions ask the Holy Spirit to direct you. It may be helpful to ask someone to pray with you. You may want to consider:

Repentance – 2 Corinthians 7:10

Repentance means to realign our thinking with God's thoughts about us and to renounce, to give up, ownership of our old way of thinking. The theologian Tom Wright reminds us that to repent is to not only "to say 'sorry', but actually in mind and action turn around in the opposite direction."[15]

We are to align our self-identity with the truth of God's word.

Part of repentance is being sorrowful for how you have lived in agreement with fear and the lies of the enemy, and for self-judgment and criticism.

Repentance acknowledges the building of your own safety strategies: protecting your 'self' rather than letting God be your Protector. It will involve renouncing or letting go of any vows or promises previously made to self-protect. It acknowledges listening to other voices rather than God's.

In essence repentance says we are sorry for taking charge and being 'ruler' over our own lives. (Remember 'Mrs. Self-reliant.)

As part of repentance we resolve not to continue living in fear and trusting in other sources for one's security, acceptance and significance. Let's remember though that this is a journey of recovery and not a one off transformation!

As we reflect on life circumstances it is important to note that we are not responsible for the behaviour of others towards us, but we are responsible for our reactions.

It is always good to ask God for a new revelation of who he is and of his love for you.

---

[15] Acts for Everyone: Part 1 by Tom Wright: page 60

Forgiveness – Matthew 6:12

"There is a hard law ... that when a deep injury is done to us, we never recover until we forgive." [16]

It is well known that forgiveness or letting go of hurts and wounds has positive psychological benefits; indeed forgiveness affects our physical, emotional and spiritual well-being and therefore our self-identity. However, forgiveness can be a hard and deep road to walk.

Forgiveness is a journey that involves pardoning those who may have caused personal hurt.

This may be a difficult journey for some particularly when there has been deep and significant hurt, for example if low self-evaluation is a result of childhood trauma or abuse. It may initially be a request; 'God help me to forgive!' (Please note, to forgive does not mean it was okay for the event to happen, it does not mean that accountability on behalf of the perpetrator is dismissed.)

Johann Christoph Arnold in 'The Lost Art of Forgiving' says, "forgiveness is the way to peace and happiness. It is also a mystery, and unless we seek it, it will remain hidden from us." [17]

Forgiveness requires action and it requires a choice. Once you are at the door of forgiveness you must open the door and walk through it. Forgiveness can be a challenging road

---

[16] Alan Paton (South African Novelist) in The Lost Art of Forgiving

[17] Johann Christoph Arnold in The Lost Art of Forgiving

to walk for those who have suffered deep wounds, but it is possible.

It is important to understand what forgiveness is, or is not, in order to decide whether to pursue it.

Forgiveness is:

- A choice to be made. It comes from the recognition that we are all human and imperfect in our 'shared humanity'. Hurt people, hurt people. It is often from a place of being hurt that we hurt others. In other words in some circumstances we have wounded people and in others we have been wounded.

  "It is impossible to forgive unless we recognize our own need for forgiveness."[18]

  To not forgive leads to resentment, the seeking of revenge, to hatred and to bitterness of soul. Not to forgive keeps the offended individual imprisoned.

- To forgive does not mean that we pretend the wounding and hurt did not happen. Healing demands an honest telling of the story and a naming of the hurts that occurred. It requires honesty and courage, it is not okay for someone to be wounded, to be abused, mistreated, beaten, or violated.

---

[18] The Lost Art of Forgiving: Accepting Responsibility: Page 122

- To forgive is an invitation to find healing, reconciliation and peace.

- Forgiveness is a personal journey that does require patience and practice.

- There is no time limit to forgiveness. It may occur in a moment or may take a prolonged period of time.

- As deep as the personal wounding and hurt might be it is important to recognise there is no person that is beyond redemption, there is no person beyond forgiveness. However, each person will have to give account for his or her actions.

Desmond and Mpho Tutu in 'The Book of Forgiving' say forgiveness is choosing to heal by:

a) Telling the story

b) Naming the hurts

c) Granting forgiveness which is done from a place of shared humanity

d) Renewing or releasing the relationship.

Forgiveness is not:

- Forgiveness does not mean that we do not grieve or get angry over what occurred. It is important to express the anger but not become captive to it.

- Forgiveness is not weakness.

- Forgiveness is not easy. When we have been deeply hurt and wounded forgiveness can seem too remote, too difficult. Why? Because to forgive means we have to face the loss and pain of what has been suffered.

- Forgiveness is not passive but requires action.

- Forgiveness is not forgetting what happened, but is a journey through cycles of remembering the story in order to face what needs to be grieved in order to enable healing.

- Forgiveness does not eliminate the memories. Painful memories will still arise and each time a choice will need to be made to believe that forgiveness is the way to healing.

Reflection Time

How would your life be different if you chose to forgive?

How would your relationships be different: with self, others, and God.

Judgment

Low self-esteem can be significantly maintained by self-criticism, self- judgments and by self-prejudicial thoughts. It is important that we:

a) Renounce, that is give up ownership of, our role as judge and jury of 'self.'

b) We may need to repent of:

- Our previous agreement(s) with our critical, judgmental, self-prejudicial thoughts and for taking on the role of Judge.

- The harm we have done to 'self.'

- For standing in opposition to the truth of what God says about us as a human being.

Healing and comfort – Acts 10:38, Psalm 119:76, Isaiah 61

God is the God of the past, present and future. Ask the Holy Spirit to come into those painful, sometimes biased memories. Ask for healing and restoration: a new perspective. God longs to bring the great exchange:

'Beauty for ashes, joy instead of mourning, praise instead of despair.' *Isaiah 61: 3*

It is helpful when praying to name all the hurting emotions: fear, anxiety, guilt, shame, anger, rejection etc. Imagine giving those hurts to Jesus.

Delivered from all our fears – Psalm 34

The Bible has some 365 references relating directly and indirectly to fear, one for each day of the year! These range from 'do not be afraid', to 'do not fear', to 'do not let your hearts be troubled'. Remember Satan wants mankind to live in fear!

Ask God to fill you to overflowing with his love which drives out all fear. Remember to ask Him to be the very source of your 'self' identity. Ask God to enable your roots, the core of your identity, to be found by going deep, deep, deep down into the soil of God's marvelous love rather than fear. *1 John 4:18, Ephesians 3:15*

When asking the question, 'who am I?' remember:

"I am a child of God, an heir." *Galatians 4:7 (Personalised)*

"I am adopted." *Ephesians 1:5 (Personalised)*

"I am loved. I cannot be separated from God's love." *Romans 8: 28 (Personalised)*

"I am complete in Christ." *Colossians 2:9-10 (Personalised)*

"I have direct access to God the Father through Jesus Christ." *Hebrews 4:14 (Personalised)*

"I have not been given a spirit of fear but of power, love and a sound mind." *2 Timothy 1:7 (Personalised)*

"I am God's workmanship." *Ephesians 2:10 (Personalised)*

"I can approach God with freedom and confidence." *Ephesians 3:12 (Personalised)*

Knowing God

In Paul's letter to the Ephesians he talks about the importance of growing in our knowledge of God. Indeed may we all know more about, and grow in, our knowledge of God. *Ephesians 1:17*

The key is to know God personally and relationally. Knowing someone and knowing about someone is different. If we are in a relationship there is an ongoing learning about the person as we get to know them. So it is with God; this is a relationship that is ever developing and growing. There is a need to take time to listen to the significant voice of God and he longs to hear from us too! As we know more of who God is, so we get to know him better. Remember relationships need nurturing.

As we come to the end of Module 3 let us take heed of the encouragement to 'Fix your thoughts on what is true and honourable and right. Think about things that are pure and lovely and admirable. Think about things that are excellent and praise worthy.' *Philippians 4:8*

Reflection Time

When God made each part of creation, 'God saw that it was good.' God made mankind; 'in the image of God he created him, male and female he created them,' and he saw they were *very good, excellent in every way*. God looks at each of us and He sees us as His children, excellent workmanship in every way.

Do you really believe this truth about your 'self'?

Model of how low self-esteem is maintained

It is important to understand how low self-evaluation is maintained in order to understand how change can be effected. Take a moment to consider how the model could be applied to yourself.

Simmering low self-evaluation:

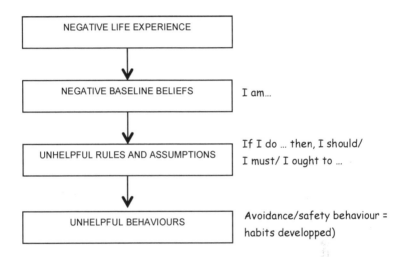

Acute low self-evaluation:

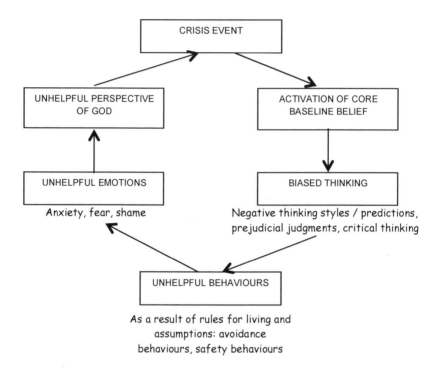

HOME ACTIVITY

As you evaluate Module 3 consider how your thinking processes hinder the re-thinking of your identity: 'who I really am.'

- Take time to review each exercise task.

- Take time to reflect on how low self-esteem has impacted your relationship with God.

- Consider asking someone to pray and journey with you as you take steps toward a healthy self-perception.

- What are you going to take away and act on from Module 3?

Summary of Module 3

- There are daily activities that maintain our negative core baseline beliefs long after the experiences involved in their formation have passed.

- Low self-esteem is maintained by what we give attention to and our biased interpretation and perception of events.

- Low self-esteem is maintained by our biased thinking styles and our prejudicial self-judgments.

- When a critical event occurs our unhelpful rules for living and assumptions are at risk of failing, with the risk that our negative core baseline beliefs will be activated.

- Unhelpful behaviours are generated from potential critical events.

⚮ In the long term avoidance maintains low self-evaluation because the fear behind the anticipatory anxiety, what we fear may happen, is never disconfirmed.

⚮ Safety behaviours appear to make the situation easier but in fact make them more difficult because they maintain the fears.

⚮ Remember that as you seek to know more of your true self and to break negative cycles, your help comes from the Lord who watches over you. *Psalm 121*

⚮ Restoration to our true sense of being is found in relationship with God and our sense of well-being develops as we discover more about our true identity: who 'I am' in Christ. Over time we will live from a place of rest, knowing we are intrinsically significant, secure and accepted.

NOTES

Whatever is true, whatever is noble, whatever is right, whatever is pure, whatever is lovely, whatever is admirable – if anything is excellent or praise worthy – think about such things.

Philippians 4:8

Module 4

Negative Thoughts and Low Self-esteem

We were created by a God who enjoys loving us, and He designed us to need this assurance from Him. When we understand the truth of God's enjoyment, our hearts become strong and bold in response. [19]

---

[19] The Seven Longings of the Human Heart by Mike Bickle with Deborah Hiebert: page 26

I am chosen and adopted

Ephesians 1: 4 & 5

Introduction

Module 3 explored why negative beliefs about ourselves persist sometimes long after the experiences involved in their formation have past. The module discussed how negative beliefs about the 'self' are maintained.

Module 4 will now explore in more detail the impact of our thought life on our identity. Many of us give little attention to what passes through our minds at any given point. The mind refers to our intellect and is the seat of our reflective consciousness, displayed through thought, perception, imagination, memories, understanding, judging and determining; all of which have emotional and behavioural responses.

Therefore what you think influences your whole life. So the question has to be asked; are your thoughts helpful and do they result in a sense of well-being or are they negative and detrimental to your sense of well-being? One could further ask; are your daily thoughts as you awaken and journey through the day generally positive or negative?

This module will particularly focus on thought(s). The Concise Oxford Dictionary defines thought as a process or power of thinking. Thought is the way of thinking characteristic to a person. (Remember Biased thinking styles in Module 2: Catastrophizing, personalising, all or nothing thinking etc.) We often hear someone refer to a train of thought or in other words what one thinks, one's opinions. A thought is the subject of one's thinking.

Thoughts can be likened to internal speech. The thoughts that go through our minds have behavioural manifestations and emotional responses. It is NOT the event or circumstance that determines how a person behaves or responds emotionally, but the thoughts, meanings, appraisals, and interpretations that the person brings to the situation or event.

Exercise task 1

Consider for a moment how your thoughts influence your core value and your sense of 'self'. This will be evidenced by what you say to your 'self 'about your 'self': how you compare your-self to others, how compassionate you are to your 'self.'

What is your appraisal or general evaluation of 'self'?

....

....

....

....

....

How does that evaluation and those thoughts affect your emotional and behavioural responses? (Remember Avoidant / Safety behaviours.)

A- Your emotional responses:

Remember avoidance does not only apply to our behavioural responses, there may be avoidance of thinking about feelings, leading to a low ability to recognise and articulate emotions.

....
....
....
....
....

B-   Your behavioural responses:

....
....
....
....
....

What is your appraisal or evaluation of how God perceives you?

....
....
....
....
....

It is helpful to note that we are on a journey of recovery and discovery, we are learning to re-think our identity. Many have spent years paying little or no attention to their thought biases; just as a physical journey takes time, so does the renewing of our minds. Romans 12: 2 encourages us that God wants to help transform us into new people by changing the way we think. Transformation always brings change. For some this will mean challenging habits of a lifetime. Let us remember that thoughts are often an opinion NOT fact, and opinions about 'self' can be transformed.

This module will focus on transforming our thoughts and thinking process regarding self-identity.

The impact of negative thoughts and renewal of the mind

We have established that low self-esteem is the term used when we have a low evaluation of 'self' and that it is maintained through negative biased thinking processes.

Some of the consequences of low self-esteem are:

- A negative view of 'self' which affects our whole sense of being and well- being, including our relationships with 'self,' others, and God.

- A difficulty in identifying personal positive qualities.

- A cycle of reinforcing the negative thoughts held against the 'self.'

- A possible avoidance of thinking about feelings, leading to a lower ability to recognise and articulate identified emotions: that is, to name emotions. (Some may refer to this as emotional intelligence.)

- Often a distorted perception of God and how God perceives us.

Few of us give adequate attention to our 'thought life' compared to our outward physical life. Consider when you get up in the morning. How often are you aware of what you are thinking at any given moment? How much more attention do you give to your outward adornment than your thoughts. Because thoughts can be so automatic, they occur and often there has been no evaluation of their content.

Low self-esteem, the low evaluation a person holds of 'self', is maintained by the vicious cycle of negative thinking and self-criticism and may include biased fear-based predictions/expectations of what may happen in a given event.

In order to renew our minds about our self-perception we need to identify these often automatic negative thoughts that on first appearance may seem logical and understand how they affect us.

Bill Johnson, author and Pastor of Bethel church in Redding, California describes the mind as a 'gatekeeper'; it is the essential tool in bringing Godly reality to the problems and challenges we face on a daily basis. As our minds are being renewed we will know increasing emotional health.

The more we let God take up residence in our lives and listen to what he has to say about our self-identity, that we are made in his image, are significant, accepted and secure in Christ, the more he can transform us by changing the way we think. Those who trust God's action in their lives find that God's Spirit is in them and that he, by the Holy Spirit, renews our daily thinking processes.

The result of living in relationship with Jesus Christ is that his peace will guard our hearts and minds. *Philippians 4:7, 1 Corinthians 2:16, Colossians 3:2, Romans 8:6, Romans 12:1-2*

What then does it mean to renew our minds? It means that we acknowledge that our current thought processes can be unhelpful to us, that they are not life giving! To renew our minds means to exchange the old unhelpful, life distorting thoughts for thoughts that are based in the truth of who we are 'in Christ.'

Before our minds are renewed our thoughts are often harmful and produce negative reactions which affect emotional and behavioural responses. Negative thinking maintains low self-esteem by contributing to the cycle of negativity or self-criticism. Unhelpful self-critical thoughts stand in opposition to the truth of who God says we are. The thoughts may initially appear logical, but as they are evaluated, disputed and challenged we can discover they are not logical and distort the truth of our identity.

In order to be able to have a greater understanding of our true self-identity (who am I?) it is necessary to:

- Identify our negative thinking

- Identify our biased fear-based predictions

- Identify our unhelpful self-critical thoughts

- Learn how to challenge our negative thinking

- Gain a new understanding of how we are made in God's image

- Renew our thinking and re-think self-identity.

As we progress on this journey of identifying negative thinking processes it may be helpful to review the difference between thoughts and feelings. It is sometimes difficult to distinguish thoughts from feelings.

Negative thoughts and feelings

Thoughts

Thoughts are a way of thinking, characteristic to a person. Often a thought is expressed as a sentence. We have established that thoughts are the running commentary on life. Thoughts can be positive or negative. When negative they are often self-critical and involve negative predictions. Thoughts can sometimes take the form of images. A person may struggle to put their thoughts into words but may have a strong image in their mind.

Automatic negative thoughts can be:

- Presented as a verbal sentence or in the form of an image.

- Appear plausible, especially when linked with strong emotional responses. However this does not make them fact.

- Are distorted because they do not take account of all the evidence. (Remember negative biased thinking styles.)

- They are subjective; they are only experienced and known by the person.

- They will often have repetitive content and themes for the person.

- They may happen in certain situations or under certain conditions.

Feelings

Emotions are expressed as feelings. They are often expressed in one word and are the affective state of our consciousness. Emotions are not reason based and people may experience a range of emotions that will differ in intensity. A feeling is the emotional side of someone's character which will be manifested in one's behaviours. It is important as individuals to identify and then to 'process' emotions in order to make sense of them. The more we manage our uncomfortable and overwhelming feelings rather than allowing the negative feelings to manage us, the more our self-esteem will improve.

For example:

'I feel ugly' does not make you ugly and does not need to rule behavioural responses.

'I feel fat' does not make you fat and does not need to rule behavioural responses.

'I feel useless' does not make you useless and does not need to rule behavioural responses.

'I feel like a failure' does not make you a failure and does not need to rule behavioural responses.

Example of self-evaluation of a negative feeling:

'I am feeling rejected because I assumed I was not being listened to in the conversation, so I withdrew.' (Note how the feeling of rejection then had a consequence on the behaviour).

To have a healthy emotional self-evaluation it is necessary for an individual:

- To learn to identify and name the emotion that is producing the feeling(s).

- To acknowledge the emotion and feeling: E.g. 'I just feel rejected, really low and sad.'

- To be able to link the emotion to the crisis event that triggered the feelings in order to give them some meaning.

- To be able to manage the emotion, that is, to decide what needs to be done in response to the feeling. Because you feel an emotion does not make it a fact.

(Remember 'personalising': because one feels something it does not make it true!)

- To be aware that because we are made in the image of God, spiritual development and awareness enhances knowledge of 'self' and others. We can learn to talk to God about personal emotions both positive and negative. The book of Psalms helps us know how to do this. Gaining a new perception of God's view of 'self –identity' is vital to our sense of being and well-being.

Allender and Longman state that: "every emotion is a theological statement.". [20]In other words, our emotions will reflect the status of our relationship with God.

- To know 'self' is not gained through turning inward but by turning outwards to God's love and exchanging negative attitudinal patterns for the truth of His words.

- It is important that we do not avoid dealing with our painful emotions. Sigmund Freud said, "Unexpressed emotions will never die. They are buried alive and will come forth later in uglier ways."

Negative emotions are not to be buried away as though dead. If the pain of rejection, guilt, anger, bitterness have not been identified, acknowledged, and given meaning from an

---

[20] Cry of the Soul by Allender and Longman: 1994

earlier event, they will fester and become manifest in another form such as low self- esteem, depression, anger, anxiety or indeed occasionally physical illness.

Healthy self-esteem means that we no longer need to run away from or avoid our negative emotions. It is important to acknowledge the feeling and to make a choice not to hide it from your 'self', others or God; 'I am feeling sad,' 'I am feeling angry.'

At this point I would like to bring a small challenge to the Church. So often I have met a resistance to Christians paying attention to what they are feeling as a part of discipleship, a part of 'denying self'.

Peter Scazzero with Warren Bird state:

"There are many other important issues related to maturing in Christ, but an honest examination of our emotions and feelings is central. This inward look is not to encourage a self-absorbed introspection that feeds narcissism".

They encourage us to look beneath the surface:

"The end result will be that you and I will be better lovers of God and other people."[21]

Remember that God's perception of us is that we are accepted, significant and loved. The Psalms are full of the Psalmist expressing a range of emotions that differed in intensity. This enables us to learn to approach God with

---

[21] The Emotionally Healthy Church by Peter Scazzero with Warren Bird: Principle 1: Look Beneath the Surface: Chapter 5: page 78

confidence and to accept ourselves and others; it is part of learning to love your neighbour as yourself. Let the knowledge of God's love for you cover everything you say and feel about your 'self'.

For some, learning to recognise and articulate emotions will be a totally new concept and may initially be like learning a new language, it may feel exhausting and even puzzling. Some are afraid of the intensity of their newly found feelings that have been buried for so long, whilst others will be further ahead on their journey of emotional discovery. Wherever you might be on the continuum of emotional discovery and recovery, be encouraged that there are huge benefits to be gained as you know more of your emotional 'self'.

As part of this journey of recovery we need to learn how to differentiate our own thoughts from our feelings; we can do this based on our earlier definition of what differentiates thoughts from feelings.

Exercise task 2

Have a go at deciding which of the following is a thought or feeling.

	Thought	Feeling
Anger	☐	☐
I don't know what to do	☐	☐
I'm frightened I will get it wrong	☐	☐
Lonely	☐	☐
I am so weary of it all	☐	☐
Depressed	☐	☐
A young woman was a little sad	☐	☐
Guilty	☐	☐

Exercise task 3

Remembering that thoughts, processes of thinking, appraisals and judgments have a consequence on our emotional responses; consider what feelings may result from the following thoughts.

Thought	Feeling
I always let myself down.	
I so enjoy going to parties.	
I know I am accepted.	
We didn't show affection in our family.	
I am so useless.	

Being able to separate thoughts from feelings is important as it initiates the first step in identifying negative thoughts. It is very difficult to have a helpful thought and a negatively linked emotional response to that thought. The consequence of a negative thought is usually a negative emotional response. The negative emotional response then serves to maintain the initial negative thought. The cycle repeats and will in turn affect our behavioural responses.

Crisis Event: Negative/ unhelpful thought response = resulting negative emotions + negative behavioural response (avoidant or safety behaviours).

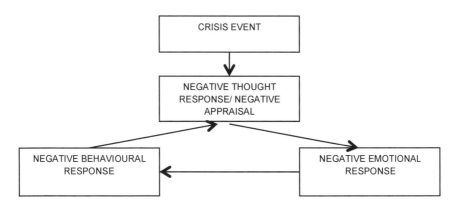

Positive Event: Positive helpful thought response = resulting positive emotions + positive behavioural response (attending).

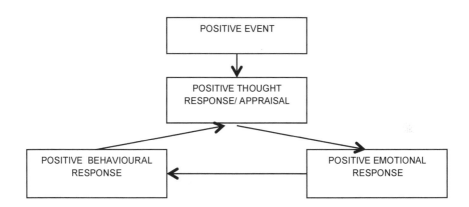

In order to challenge our negative thinking and renew our minds, it is needful to be more aware of our thoughts in daily life. As we identify our negative thinking we will become aware of old habitual thought patterns.

Exercise task 4

Consider an event that was difficult for you. Note down your responses identifying what you thought, and how you responded emotionally and behaviourally.

Difficult / crisis event

....

↓

Negative thought/ negative
appraisal

....

....

Negative behavioural response   Negative emotional response

....

....

←

Consider an event that was positive for you. Note down your responses identifying what you thought, and how you responded emotionally and behaviourally.

Positive event

....

↓

Positive thought/ appraisal

....

....

Positive behavioural response   Positive emotional response

....   ←   ....

....

Exercise task 5

To enable identification of negative thinking it is helpful to keep a journal.

Identify your negative thinking over the next week keep a journal noting down your negative thoughts and the emotional and behavioural consequences. Note the impact on your relationship with God.

Events	Thought/ Image	Emotional response	Behavioural response	Response to God

On completing the record what did you notice or learn about your responses? (Patterns of thinking; use of biased thinking styles; did your behaviour link to your rules for living?)

....

....

....

....

....

Negative thoughts and biased fear-based predictions / expectations

Low self-esteem and the low evaluation a person holds about 'self' is maintained by the vicious cycle of negative thinking and may include biased memories, and self-criticism. This low self-esteem can be referred to as *'simmering'* low self-evaluation. At any given moment this negative cycle greatly influences and distorts the answer to the question of 'self-identity: who am I?'

Someone with a low self-esteem may be living at the level of *'simmering'* low self-evaluation until a crisis event occurs. This will then trigger an 'acute' low self-evaluation episode.

In a crisis event, a person's negative self-perception such as: 'I am useless', 'I am pathetic', can trigger existing biased fearful predictions / expectations; that is, what they anxiously predict / expect will happen in the crisis event, almost like self-fulfilling prophecy.

We have already stated that life is full of unexpected daily challenges which may be interpreted through the lens of our negative core baseline beliefs and unhelpful rules for living and assumptions. Remember that crisis events are a crucial time when 'rules for living' ('I should do, I must do, I ought to') and 'assumptions' ('If I do … then …') are at threat of being broken. This is inevitable because rules and assumptions are inflexible, unrealistic and too high to live up to.

Unexpected challenges become possible crisis events when simmering low self-esteem can become more acute because the biased fear based predictions / expectations are at threat of failing.

Let's look at an example of a *'Simmering'* low self-evaluation becoming an 'acute' low self-evaluation:

CASE STUDY: Mr England

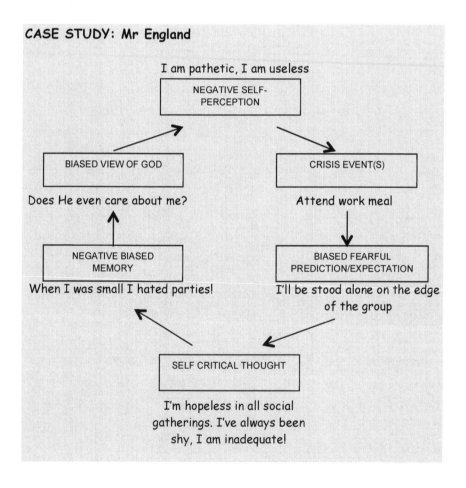

When a crisis event happens Mr. England experiences a very real difficulty in living up to his set of 'rules for living' or avoiding his assumptions. For example one of Mr. England's 'rule for living' was:

'I make it a policy not to attend work social functions.'

The crisis event brought an inability for Mr. England to keep this rule or to avoid the threat of his assumption:

'If I go to a social event I will not be able to maintain a conversation or will be stood on the edge of the group not feeling part of the gathering and so will appear totally inadequate.'

The result for Mr. England was an acute low self-evaluation.

His negative core baseline belief about his sense of 'self' was activated:

'I am pathetic,' 'I am useless.'

This influenced his thinking processes and emotional and behavioural responses. For example, when Mr. England's rule for living looked as though it was about to be broken and his response was to anxiously predict or expect that things would turn out badly, he was creating biased fear based predictions / expectations:

'I'll be stood alone on the edge of the group.'

This resulted in self-critical thoughts:

'I'm hopeless in all social gatherings.'

'I've always been shy.'

'I am inadequate'!

Mr. England's negative thinking biases caused him to start catastrophizing and personalising further. They were unhelpful in that they further maintained his negative thinking and caused him to start jumping to conclusions. Note how biased memories were recalled:

'When I was small I hated parties!'

These resulted in biased fearful predictions / expectations:

'I'll be stood alone on the edge of the group.'

Consequently Mr. England started to alter his behaviours by becoming cautious and over-rehearsing possible conversations (employing safety behaviours). His thoughts and behaviours contributed to his increased anxiety, fear and self-doubt which in turn confirmed to him his core baseline belief: 'I am pathetic'. This in turn affected his relationship with God as he started to see all the 'giants' before him.

Mr. England's *'simmering'* low self-evaluation had become an *'acute'* low self-evaluation triggered by a crisis event: he had to attend a work meal that he previously had avoided at all cost.

It is important to start identifying the biased fearful predictions made in a crisis event in order to begin challenging them.

Exercise task 6

Identifying biased predictions / expectations

Over the next week keep a 'thought record' in your journal.

Each day record any difficult or crisis event/s, the negative predictions made, and the result of these predictions on your emotions and behaviours.

What was the crisis event?

....

....

....

....

....

What biased fear-based predictions / expectations regarding the event were made? (What did you think would happen?)

....

....

....

....

....

How much did you believe the negative prediction / expectation? (Rate belief 0-100%)

....

....

....

....

....

Identify the felt emotion/s? (Rate the intensity 0-100%)

....

....

....

....

....

What action was taken to stop the negative prediction / expectation coming true? (Avoidant / safety behaviours employed

....

....

....

....

....

How did your negative prediction/ expectation impact your relationship with God?

....

....

....

....

....

How did your negative predictions / expectations link with your core baseline belief statements? (I am)

....

....

....

....

....

It is necessary to acknowledge that low self-esteem is maintained by fear-based anxiety. The fear is that the 'rules for living and assumptions' put in place to protect self-identity may be in danger of being broken or even of failing when a difficult or crisis event occurs.

Fear can paralyse or cause severe limitations to personal freedom. Mr. England never wanted to go to a work function because of fear. We can become a 'slave' to the fears manifest in our negative thinking. We can become so bound to our negative predictions and expectations that life becomes limited and we do not live out of the fullness of our identity.

As we progress in getting to know God it is important to acknowledge that being a slave to negative thinking happens when we have no foundational truth or have lost, or are losing sight of the truth of how God perceives us. We are tempted to accept distorted ideas and beliefs about the identity of 'self' and often use these substitutes to build the sense of 'self' that can never satisfy, but rather will lead us further away from freedom.

As part of the journey taken in challenging low self-evaluation regular appraisals are required to help assess whose significant voice is being held as most important. We must consider whose significant voice is readily and regularly listened to and is believed to be true, and what the resulting wounding messages may be to our 'self' identity. Typically our answers will cover the examples below:

- The negative 'self' with all the anxious fear-filled predictions and expectations.

- The negative significant internalised voices from earlier childhood or adult trauma experiences.

- Our adversary, the devil who prowls around like a roaring lion.

- God: His purpose is to give life in all its fullness, but our misinterpretation of God's action or perceived inaction, may lead us to believe otherwise.

Fear kills and steals and needs to be challenged head on!

It is important to remember that negative thoughts and predictions / expectations are often opinions rather than facts. This means we can dispute and challenge them rather than just become a slave to them and the distress they may bring. To challenge our negative thought predictions / expectations means:

- To evaluate how accurate or likely they are to happen.

- To look for the evidence that the negative prediction / expectation is based on.

- To identify any positives that are being ignored or disregarded.

- To reassess how we perceive our relationship with God.

Once you have started to identify your negative biased predictions / expectations in your 'thought record' you will then be ready to commence the step by step process of challenging the biased predictions / expectations.

Exercise task 7

Challenging your biased predictions/ expectations

The following questions may help you to use your journal to complete the thought record below:

What is the evidence for my biased fear-based prediction / expectation regarding the event?

What is the evidence against my biased fear-based prediction / expectation regarding the event?

On a scale of 0-10 how likely is it that what I am predicting / expecting will happen?

What is the worst that could happen?

What is the best that could happen?

What is the most likely thing that will happen?

How else could I view this situation?

If the worst happens, what could I do to help myself?

What are the positives I am ignoring?

How am I involving God in my thought battle?

Using the questions have a go at completing your thought record:

What is the crisis event / difficult situation?

....
....
....
....
....

What is your biased fear based prediction / expectation regarding the event? What am I thinking will happen?

....
....
....
....
....

How much do I believe it will happen? (Rate belief 0-100%)

....

What are the felt emotion/s? (Rate the intensity 0-100%)

....
....

....
....
....

What is an alternative realistic view to this situation? Use the questions to find an alternative realistic perspective of the situation. (Rate belief 0-100%)

....
....
....
....
....

Experiment

1. What did you do instead of taking precautions?

....
....
....
....
....

2. Re-rate the intensity of your emotions that you were originally feeling. (0-100%)

....
....
....
....
....

3. How much do you now believe your original biased prediction / expectation (0-100%)?

....
....
....
....
....

3.1. What was it like to act differently?

....
....
....
....
....

3.2. What did you learn?

....
....
....
....
....

3.3. What were the positives that you were ignoring / disregarding? (Your strengths and qualities?)

....
....
....
....
....

3.4. How did your new alternative perspective impact your relationship with God?

....
....

....

....

....

3.5. How does challenging your biased predictions / expectations alter your core baseline beliefs about 'self'? (Your 'I am' statements)

....

....

....

....

....

Biased predictions / expectations occur when we are afraid that our Rules for Living ('I should do, I must do, and I ought to') or assumptions ('If I do ... then ...') that defend against the pain of our negative core baseline beliefs about the 'self', are in danger of failing or being broken. Biased predictions / expectations overestimate the possibility that something bad will occur and underestimate one's ability to cope.

By identifying and challenging theses negative thought predictions and expectations, renewal of the mind occurs, enabling the individual to disconfirm personal fears.

As we invite God to help us in this process and trust his action in our lives by the work of his Spirit, a spiritual renewal of thoughts and attitude takes place and a new person created in God's likeness emerges. *Ephesians 4:23*

We have explored the origins of simmering low self-evaluation, and how it is maintained and is then triggered to become acute low self-evaluation.

We have also acknowledged that when an individual encounters a difficult / crisis event, core baseline negative beliefs ('I am' statements) are activated which can lead to two types of negative thoughts:

- Biased fear-based predictions / expectations

- Self-critical thinking.

In order to continue our journey to answer the self-identity question 'who am I?' the next module will explore how it is now necessary to combat unhelpful self-critical thinking. This continues to involve the renewing of the mind as we develop a more balanced and truthful view of the 'self' and learn to accept our true self-identity.

HOME ACTIVITY

- Take some time to reflect on how your negative thinking influences your self-identity on a daily basis.

- What has been the past consequence of your low self-evaluation on your 'self', others, your relationship with God and on your daily living activities?

- Review the difference between thoughts and feelings.

- Note a circumstance when 'simmering' low self-evaluation became 'acute' low self-evaluation: what impact did biased fear based predictions / expectations have on the process?

- Take time to journal with God about how He perceives you.

- What are you going to take away and act on from Module 4?

Summary of module 4

🕭 Thoughts can be likened to internal speech.
What we think and the thoughts that go
through our minds have behavioural
manifestations and emotional responses.

🕭 Few of us give adequate attention to our
'thought life' compared to our outward physical
life.

🕭 Low self-esteem, the low evaluation a person
holds of 'self', is maintained by the vicious cycle
of negative thinking and self-criticism and may
include biased fear-based predictions /
expectations of what may happen in a given
event.

- Healthy self-esteem means that we no longer need to run away from or avoid our negative emotions. It is important to acknowledge the feeling and to make a choice not to hide from your 'self', others or God.

- Biased predictions / expectations overestimate the possibility that something bad will occur and underestimate one's ability to cope.

- Remember this journey is a walk of faith. Walking by faith can lead to a life of faith.

NOTES

That you, being rooted and established in love, may have power, together with all the saints, to grasp how wide and long and high and deep is the love of Christ, and know this love that surpasses knowledge.

Ephesians 3:19

Module 5

Self-critical Thinking

In His presence, my masks fall off, my false selves are revealed. I stand stripped and naked before Him. To continually abide in His presence is to have one face only – the true one. To draw near Him, therefore, is to find the real 'I' as well as its true home, my true center. [22]

---

[22] The Healing Presence by Leanne Payne: Page 72

I am loved with an everlasting love

Jeremiah 31:3 (adapted)

Introduction

As already acknowledged, the sense of 'self' and how self-identity is perceived is influenced by many external factors such as family, culture, social and political expectations and the spiritual beliefs we hold and practice. All affect self-identity and one's sense of well-being.

In the west we live in a culture where the social mode is to assess each individual from birth. We are consistently assessed according to achievement and what we do. We are very often productivity orientated. Our society is filled with developmental performance expectations and behavioural audits.

From infancy and throughout the adult working life we are expected to improve performance with talk of audits in many and varied forms; school pupils are consistently assessed for achievement targets and adults must comply with company behaviours. Indeed, in most spheres of working life we are expected to meet audit standards and so it goes on through all areas of society: all are required to 'do', with the obligation to work harder for the sake of productivity. These expectations are often internalised by the individual and then reinforced in family, social groupings, church and national identities.

In the light of society's expectations and our earliest childhood experiences, we learn to make life appraisals and endeavour to determine the answer to the 'self' identity question 'who am I?' We each have a need to feel secure and feel significant with a sense of worth. Our motivation is to be appreciated and loved as an individual.

The internal beliefs formed and held by an individual about themselves as a result of these sometimes pressured expectations, combined with early life experiences, are key factors in our self-evaluation.

A healthy self-evaluation is illustrated when we know that we are valuable and can speak well of ourselves, when we are able to 'just be' and have a sense of steadiness in our lives whatever the challenges.

Self-critical thoughts

We have already defined 'self' to be a person's individuality, or essence. To be critical means to be fault finding. Therefore to be self-critical means to be fault finding, to be censorious of one's individuality, of the essence of 'self', of the core of one's 'self-identity'.

To be self-critical is the equivalent to having an internal task master that punishes 'self' each time 'self' does not perform or achieve a certain standard, whether standards of our own making or those of others. Often those standards are too high to achieve or the route to achievement is often not understood or even accessible. The inability to reach such standards may result in self-criticism:

'I'm hopeless', 'I am a failure', 'I will never amount to anything', 'I'm an idiot'.

Low self-evaluation is illustrated by thoughts, ideas and beliefs about the 'self' that are expressed as negative self-critical thoughts either as a personal internal commentary running through the mind, and / or as verbalised to others. These self-critical thoughts result in negative emotional and behavioural responses.

For example, self-critical thoughts can be:

'I am useless', 'I am hopeless at administration', 'I'm a bad Mum', 'I'm never going to achieve much', 'I'm stupid.'

All such thoughts can result in consequential negative emotional and behavioural responses.

For example, the repeated self- critical thought 'I'm a bad mother' might have the following consequential negative thinking biases and responses for a mother who often says this to herself as an internal running commentary. They can be like sticky labels. (See Module 3)

a) Biased self-perception: bias in how she sees her 'self'.

b) Biased interpretation: the meaning she attaches to an event.

c) Biased thinking styles: Disqualifying positives, all or nothing thinking.

d) Prejudicial thinking: biased opinion against her 'self'.

e) Rules for living and assumption may be attached to her thinking: I should, I must, and I ought to achieve certain standards. If I don't do … then I have failed.

The internal commentary held by the mother will in turn affect her relationship with her 'self' and with all her relationships including the child she cares for, others and God.

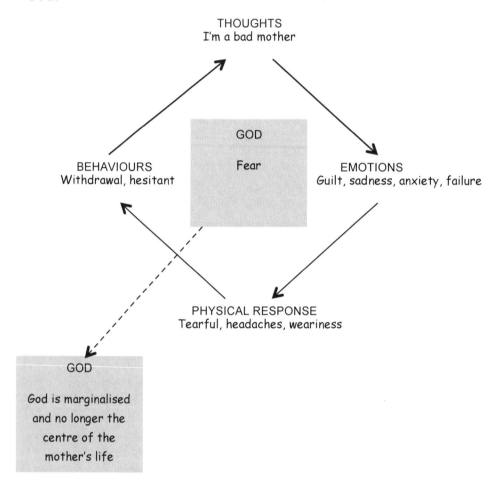

THOUGHTS
I'm a bad mother

GOD
Fear

BEHAVIOURS
Withdrawal, hesitant

EMOTIONS
Guilt, sadness, anxiety, failure

PHYSICAL RESPONSE
Tearful, headaches, weariness

GOD

God is marginalised
and no longer the
centre of the
mother's life

Over time the negative internal commentary becomes a habit of thought and may result in God becoming marginalised and fear taking centre stage.

Such thoughts diminish and hurt 'self'.

Self-critical thoughts are like a 'harsh supervisor or task master' that constantly follow you, pointing out every mistake with comments full of disapproval. Reflect for one moment: would you speak to a friend as you speak to your 'self?' Remember love your neighbour as you love your 'self'.

Self-critical thoughts are unfair and demoralising because they discount every achievement or success, which undermines confidence. In time the habit of self-criticism hinders growth and change. Self-critical thoughts are often based on the internalised critical voices of others (Module 1) and will then collude with our biased self-perception and biased interpretation of events and circumstances.

Exercise task 1

Self-critical thoughts can be evidenced either as a personal internal commentary running through the mind, and / or as verbalised to others.

Take a moment to consider:

On a scale of 0-10 how self-critical are you? 0 being the lowest - 10 being the highest.

. . . .

Consider the following to help gauge how self-critical you are when you talk to your 'self'. Note the content of 'self-talk' for each statement:

Very critical and negative, a 'harsh task master / supervisor'? Write down some of your internal commentary:

....
....
....
....
....

Fairly confident and supportive, but there are some days when the internal 'self' talk holds me back: Do you notice if there is a pattern to your negative commentary?

....
....
....
....
....

Confident and helpful, I have learned to nurture my 'self' and can identify and challenge my negative critical thoughts.

....
....
....
....
....

It is so important to acknowledge that self-critical thoughts do not align with Biblical truth; they stand in opposition to the truth of God's perception of each individual. Self-critical thoughts are the opposite of how Father God perceives each individual who is made in his image. It is to be remembered that our minds are a strategic battlefield and many wars are won and lost in our thought-life!

The effect of self-critical thinking

As we have explored, self-critical thinking is harmful and hurtful to 'self.' It is a form of grumbling against the 'self' that can eventually, if it becomes habitual, be deadly to the 'true-self'. Self-criticism keeps the 'self' in the 'shadow-lands.' Grumbling against 'self' has four consequences:

- It causes *infection:* that is, it brings disease or 'dis-ease' to the essence of self-identity: the 'who am I?' question. It affects emotional well-being, physical and behavioural responses and our relationships with self / others / God.

- It causes *disorientation:* it is a task master that argues, opposes and distorts the truth of God's perspective of each individual. It moves us away from a core resting place of acceptance, significance, and security to a place of fear and anxiety.

- It is *censorious:* it leads to fault finding and breeds self-rejection and self-judgment. It is prejudicial.

- It is *disastrous:* it significantly affects a person's relationships, well-being and daily living activities. It causes a self-forfeiting, a sabotage of the scope of God's plans for his child.

Exercise task 2

Take a moment to reflect on your grumbling against 'self': Consider the words:

Infection	Disorientation
Censorious	Disastrous

What effect is self-critical thinking having on you?

....

....

....

....

....

As already discussed, our negative self-evaluations are negative thoughts that are 'simmering' and they are especially triggered when a difficult or crisis event is encountered. It is at this point that our unhelpful Rules for Living or assumptions can be broken and the negative core baseline beliefs ('I am' statements) are activated:

'I am useless,' 'I cannot cope,' 'I am pathetic,' 'I am a failure.'

When this occurs there is a potential to evaluate 'self' negatively and critically with a tendency to:

- Respond to your *Rules for Living*: 'I should have, I ought to have', with a harsh self-punishing for not meeting up to the standards set for the 'self.'

- Activation of negative thinking biases: jumping to conclusions, personalising etc. One mistake at an event is personalised to mean, 'I am a mistake.'

- The use of double standards, condemning 'self' as a person on the basis of one event, concentrating on weaknesses and forgetting all your strengths. This can sometimes be evidenced as the perfectionist.

- The activation of biased self-prejudicial thoughts. Who needs enemies when we can punish 'self' so harshly?

- The activation of avoidant and safety behaviours.

- Protecting 'self' by using all the above strategies, rather than turning to God.

The diagram shows an example of the consequence of 'self' critical evaluation:

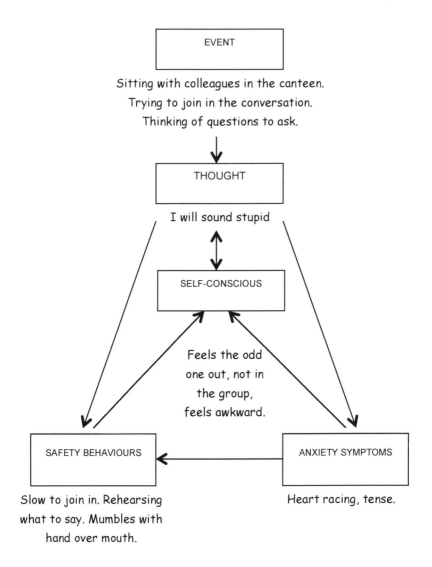

We all at times lose sight of God. We need to be alert to the truth that our adversary the devil subtly builds to influence our personal life, our thoughts, our feelings, our attitudes and behaviour patterns.

'Be self-controlled and alert. Your enemy the devil prowls around like a roaring lion looking for some-one to devour.' *1 Peter 5:8*

For example the prowl of the enemy can be in the form of discouragement, guilt or despair. His roar will be through his lies about your identity, such as: 'you are useless, you have failed again, and you are never going to change.' We need to be alert to his strategies and the patterns he uses to prowl and roar in each individual's life. Remember his aim is to steal, kill and destroy your identity.

When thoughts become so self-critical, there is a negative impact on:

Emotions

Constant self-criticism may result in low mood, guilt, shame, anger, sadness, despair et al, and a sense of failure for not meeting the standard of rules set; 'I should have...... I just never get it right'. This in turn helps confirm the negative core baseline beliefs; 'I am useless' (low self-evaluation) and can result in symptoms of depression over time.

Physical responses

Self-criticism will affect our bodies. Tiredness, tension in the shoulders, headaches, weariness, tearfulness and exhaustion are not uncommon due to the inner 'dis-ease' taking place as the 'who am I?' conflict is being battled and evaluated.

Behaviours

Constant self-criticism affects confidence and one's ability to cope and make decisions. This may result in unhelpful behaviours such as withdrawing from events, isolating self, neglecting things, and not taking initiative. It may result in passivity with a lack of assertiveness with others. Self-critical thinking is a learned habit that causes harm and encourages a person to act in self-defeating, self-sabotaging ways. The key is that self-critical thoughts can prevent positive self-development and change from occurring. (See Module 3 for avoidant and safety behaviours.)

God response

Ephesians 4:23 encourages individuals to: 'be made new in the attitude of your minds'

However when difficult times are perceived, the battle in the mind can be very real and intense; a sense of suffering increases the possibility that we might doubt the sovereignty of God.

The prowl and the roar of the enemy can also influence our response to God and it is at this point that we so often remove God from the centre of our lives. This can be because:

a) We doubt our identity; who we are and how God perceives us:

'I'm not good enough, I have failed and got it wrong again.'

b) That we doubt God's identity;

'He doesn't answer my prayers, what is the point?', 'He does not listen to me', or 'why did he let that happen?' We can often find 'self' asking: 'God where are you?'

Responding in this way can open the door to increased self-criticism, when our experience in the crisis event seems to confirm the negative beliefs held about self and/ or God.

Consider for a moment, when life seems most brutal, how do you view God's sovereignty? What direction do you go in? Do you trust or doubt God's plan for you?

So often when life is difficult it feels like the event / circumstance is predominant. It is at this point that we have all at times acted as though we are sovereign. We take control because in our minds God does not seem to be acting, so we try to defend our 'self 'and make plans for survival. We de-throne the only Sovereign God.

When the hard event occurs it can affect our relationship with God and we can become more self-critical. It looks like this:

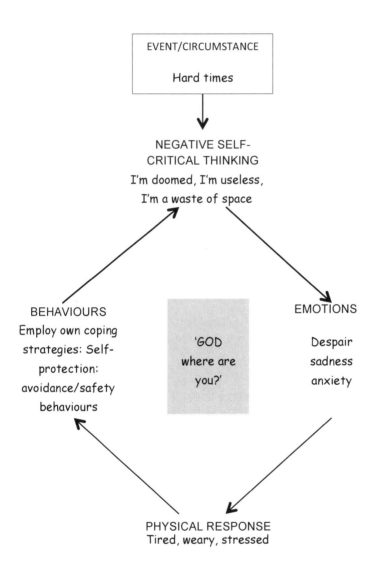

When in crisis God is often no longer at the centre of our lives; we place him in the margins because we have decided we need to take control because FEAR motivates 'self-survival / protection'.

Exercise task 3

Have a go at mapping the consequences of your 'self' critical thoughts:

Consequences of self-critical thinking:

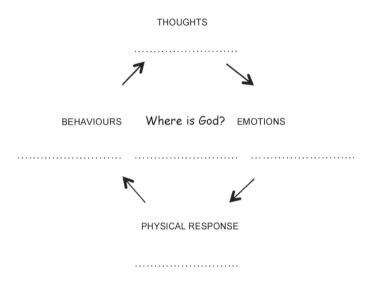

THOUGHTS

....

BEHAVIOURS   Where is God?   EMOTIONS

....

PHYSICAL RESPONSE

....

We need to remember God always has the best plan for us.

'For I know the plans I have for you, plans to prosper you and not harm you, plans to give you a hope and a future.' *Jeremiah 29:11*

As American Pastor Mark Driscoll suggests we often only see His Sovereign plan as we look in our rear view mirror! [23]

------

[23] Who Do You Think You Are? By Mark Driscoll

As we explore the effect of self-critical thinking take a minute to consider whether being harsh and self-critical about your 'self' is a helpful or unhelpful thing to do.

Exercise task 4

Have a go at mapping the consequences of your 'self' critical thoughts:

On a scale of 0 -10 how helpful is your self-critical thinking?

....

Self-criticism is helpful because:

....
....
....
....
....

Self-criticism is unhelpful because:

....
....
....
....
....

Some people do think that making negative self-evaluations is a good thing, believing it has positive motivational consequences.

Exercise task 5

It may help at this point to take time to consider the advantages and disadvantages of self-criticism in terms of the effect it has on the self-identity, 'who am I?' question.

Does self-criticism affect your sense of being and well-being?

....
....
....
....
....

Does self-criticism prevent you from doing certain things?

....
....
....
....
....

Does self-criticism affect how you feel emotionally?

....
....

....
....
....

Does self-criticism affect your relationship with God?

....
....
....
....
....

Does self-criticism align with the truth of how God perceives you?

....
....
....
....
....

Does self-criticism affect your thinking processes? (Biased thinking styles, biased self-perception etc.)

....
....
....
....
....

Exercise task 6

As you consider the advantages and disadvantages of self-critical thinking it may help to see them in a table to facilitate a direct comparison:

Advantages of self-criticism	Disadvantages of self-criticism

As we have discussed, to be constantly self-critical and making regular negative self-evaluations is unhelpful and helps to maintain low self-esteem.

It increases emotional distress with feelings of frustration, hopelessness, disappointment, guilt, despair, sadness, anger against 'self' and may lead to anxiety and or depression.

Self-criticism will affect relationship with self, others, and God. In order to help discover the truth to the 'who am I?' question it is important to re-think 'self'-critical thought(s) by:

- Identifying 'self'-critical thought(s)

- Challenging 'self'-critical thought(s)

- Re- balancing 'self'-critical thought(s)

Becoming aware of self-critical thinking

Identifying 'self' critical thought(s)

Few of us give consistent attention to our thought life and what passes through our minds, as compared to our outward practical life. For many it is often impossible to stop the mind from thinking about something. The more one tries not to think, the more the mind can be full of mental activity. Intellection describes someone who likes to think, however this mental activity can be unhelpful when it becomes the sculptor of unhelpful self-critical thoughts.

Rather than thought-removal the goal is the renewal of the mind; to learn to identify self-critical thoughts, images, and beliefs in order to challenge and take them captive. The objective is to renew or re-think the unhelpful thought in order to prevent its negative consequences on self-identity, personal well-being and relationships.

Proverbs 23:7 (KJV) says: 'As a man thinks in his heart so he is.'

Our imaginations can create either a work of art that is beautiful, or a horror movie. When the thoughts of our mind are focused on the negative, the self-critical, and the self-judgmental and on self-comparison, we are living the 'horror movie'.

It is necessary to pay attention to our mind and recognise how much time is spent brooding on unhelpful content, such as: why someone hurts you; someone else's success; one's loneliness; how unfair life can be.

Samuel Smiles wrote:

Sow a *thought* you reap an act,

Sow an *act* and you reap a habit,

Sow a *habit* and you reap a character,

Sow a *character* and you reap a *destiny*.

Exercise task 7

Ponder for a moment your self-critical thinking and the process of those words in your life:

Thought – Act – Habit – Character – Destiny

....

....

....
....
....

We can all have troubling self-critical thoughts, but the key is that we have a *choice* of what to do with them:

a) Identify the negative self-critical thought(s) and take them captive as you would an enemy,

OR

b) Identify the thought(s) and allow 'self' to feed on and indulge them!

It is a hard fact that constant self-criticism will, and does, affect our character and destiny in life. Self-criticism affects self-identity: the 'who am I?' question.

You may be aware of particular situations when self-critical thoughts, or habits of self-criticism are more prevalent. Sometimes we can surprise ourselves with how self-critical we are.

Exercise task 8

Sometimes self-criticism becomes so habitual we don't easily notice when we are being self-critical.

Keep a journal for a week

Write down trigger situations in which you are aware of being more self-critical. What were you doing when you began to feel bad about your 'self?' Notice if a pattern emerges.

....

....

....

....

....

Write down your emotional and physical responses.

....

....

....

....

....

Write down the self-critical words you use about or against your 'self'. Thoughts can be expressed in words / images / meanings.

....

....

....

....

....

If you find it difficult, ask a trusted family member / friend / colleague to point out to you each time you speak negatively about or against your 'self'. Record their comments:

....

....

....

....

....

What did you do as a result of your self-critical thoughts?

....

....

....

....

....

Did your thoughts line up with the truth of how God perceives you? (Significant, accepted, secure in His love).

....

....

....

....

....

Challenging 'self' critical thoughts: taking captive self-critical thoughts and destroying negative strongholds

Thought-life plays an important role in the way we handle life and its circumstances. The mind is expressed through our emotions and behaviours; our thoughts can produce a sense of well-being or they can produce suffering.

In the same way as we challenged our biased predictions / expectations, so too we can challenge our self-critical thoughts. It is important to remember that thoughts are often opinions, judgments and appraisals made about an event or circumstance; they are not fact. This means that once *identified* we can dispute and *challenge* the resulting self-critical thoughts that have been formed. We can then take them captive and compare them to the truth of what God says about us: *re- balance* the thought in truth. This is a process of renewing the mind.

When applied to one's self- evaluation it is a process of *re-thinking identity.*

'We demolish arguments and every pretention that sets itself up against the knowledge of God, and we take captive every thought to make it obedient to Christ.' *2 Corinthians 10:5*

The Message Bible explains it as: 'fitting every loose thought and emotion and impulse into the structure of life shaped by Christ.'

It is important to note that if anyone has formed habitual patterns, a settled tendency or practice of self-critical thought, they can become a stronghold.

A stronghold is a military term to describe a fort. A soldier builds up a barrier of protection, a wall in order to protect himself from what he perceives as danger. Self-critical thinking can become a false barrier of protection (remember safety behaviours) that can eventually become an ingrained habit and therefore a stronghold of resistance against the Godly truth of self-identity. The truth is that we are so often afraid of loneliness, of not being recognised, or of being ignored, that we develop strategies to protect our 'self' and to assure our 'self' of the love we think we deserve.

However, we are encouraged to recognise the battle taking place in our thought-life and are instructed to demolish these strongholds.

'The weapons we fight with are not the weapons of the world. On the contrary, they have divine power to demolish strongholds.' *2 Corinthians 10:4*

Strongholds can be defined as things in which human confidence is placed. These strongholds can be seen in reoccurring negative habits; it is an area of a person's life that provides shelter and strength to a pattern of thinking or to a view point. The stronghold is an argument or pretention that opposes the truth and knowledge of God.

For example:

'Things are never going to change, I'm stuck here, it is useless, there is no point trying.'

This stronghold is based on the thought/s of, 'I'm a failure', 'I'm powerless' and is rooted in self-rejection. It keeps the individual captive to a negative 'self' perception and makes them afraid to take a risk for change. It stops growth and opposes the truth of God's perception of the individual as precious and honoured and loved.

For our low self-evaluation to change it is necessary to take captive every self- critical thought that questions the truth of who you are in God; that questions your identity as loved, significant, secure and accepted.

Consider the enemy soldier who is found on the wrong side of the line, he is restrained and taken as a captive or expelled from the country. The aim in taking him captive is to prevent him from further harming or imposing damage on friendly forces.

So it is with every unhelpful and self-critical thought. The thought needs to be apprehended, restrained and either brought under control or expelled to prevent it from harming the core of who you say you are: your self-identity.

If self-critical thoughts are left to run unrestrained through the mind they undermine the very core of 'who I really am' from within.

It is important to be aware that your adversary the devil, who prowls around looking for someone to devour, joins in to help build the self-critical stronghold(s) so that he might undermine the knowledge and plans of God for your self-identity.

Personal strongholds are things that Satan has sought to build and to influence your personal life, including your thoughts, your feelings, your attitudes and behaviour patterns. We have also colluded at times with Satan in the building of these stronghold(s).

Edgardo Silvoso of Harvest Evangelism suggests: 'A stronghold is a mindset impregnated with hopelessness, that causes the believer to accept as unchangeable something that he/she knows is contrary to the will of God.'

As a stronghold is established one's self-evaluation becomes depleted.

We need to acknowledge that there is a daily war taking place – a spiritual battle for our minds.

There are *choices* to be made.

Consider for a moment the human need to be accepted, secure and significant as opposed to being rejected.

- Acceptance means to be approved, worthy, pleasing, favourable.

- Secure means untroubled by danger or apprehension. To have a secure existence, a secure dwelling. To be confident, safe against attack. To be in safe keeping.

- Significant means to have meaning, to be of real importance.

As on a continuum, some people will have known a measure of all of these, some very little indeed. The day to day, here and now, superficial knowing of acceptance, security, and significance will vary for an individual from place to place, in various relationships, and in differing circumstances.

However the true, 'deep to deep' knowing of acceptance, security, and significance in the very core of one's being and identity, is to be found in relationship with the triune God. He has made us in his image, and has made a way for us to be his adopted children, of intrinsic worth. It is this deep knowing of one's acceptance, security, and significance 'in Christ' that enables an individual to stand in the day to day hard knocks of life, and to know one's intrinsic worth without a need to achieve or to be productive in order to feel of worth.

For example, each of us at some point will have put negative thought patterns in place to protect the 'self' from the fear and consequences of anxiety caused by the possibility of perceived or actual rejection.

This in turn can become a stronghold of rejection where we anticipate the rejection of others. In the face of potential rejection we then self-reject by using self-criticism and act / behave with avoidant or safety behaviours. All of these reactions serve to maintain the stronghold and are all engineered in an attempt to self-protect against the feared rejection.

For example:

- *'I am unacceptable – I'm not likeable – I am rubbish'.*

- *'I am insecure – I don't fit – I am not like the rest - I am different'.*

- *'I am insignificant – I am the black sheep in the family - I was never as good as my brother'.*

Each of us will have sought to take control of life circumstances in order to protect and defend our self-identity from the harmful significant voices of others, the wounding messages of the world, and the resulting observations on God's character.

Remember that self-critical thoughts will be evidenced in consequential emotional and behavioural responses. Self-critical thoughts will affect our relationship with 'self', others and God.

The strongholds and habitual thought patterns of self-critical thinking that we put in place to self-protect, will ultimately control our thoughts and resulting emotional and behavioural responses. They will deceive us into believing we are something other than what we are: the 'false-self'. They will cause a conscious and at times sub conscious rejection of the truth about a loving relationship with God and a knowing of His ways.

For example, negative self-talk can intimidate us and prevent us from taking positive steps so as to avoid fear of failure.

Negative self-talk says: 'You are a failure, there is no point trying new things, you will only fail again.'

Consider the following statements:

'I am a failure': this assumes a position of failure-hood through attaching, failure to the 'self' like a sticky label. It feels constant and unchangeable, discounting any success in life. It also projects failure into the person's future. Fear of failure can prevent the person trying new things and so prevents personal growth.

'I will always be stuck, things never work out for me': This assumes a victim mentality with no hope of change and will impact the emotional well-being of the individual and behavioural responses to daily living activities. People who think this way dismiss any personal strengths or achievements. Being 'stuck in a rut' in their thinking process will make it more difficult to take risks. This stronghold of thought maintains avoidant behaviour. It prevents change and opposes the truth of how God perceives the individual.

Richard Rohr describes the false-self as the 'shadow-self'. He suggests that by protecting the 'self', we become less able to recognize our true selves, causing a form of double blindness which keeps the individual from seeing – and being – your best and deepest self. [24]

As Jesus put it, 'If the lamp within you is, in fact, darkness, what darkness there will be.' *Matthew 6:23*

As part of challenging and demolishing strongholds it is helpful to identify and recognise what our habitual self-critical thinking patterns are.

As already discussed our negative self-evaluations are negative thoughts that 'simmer' and they are especially triggered when a difficult or crisis event is encountered. It is at this point that our unhelpful Rules for Living or assumptions can be broken and the negative core baseline beliefs, or 'I am' statements are activated.

Self-critical thoughts are often evidenced by our strong emotional and behavioural responses.

---

[24] Falling Upward by Richard Rohr: 'The Shadowlands': Chapter 11: page 128

Exercise task 9

To help challenge formed strongholds consider:

When you are rejected (not accepted: not feeling approved, worthy, pleasing, favourable):

1. What do you do to protect yourself?
2. What do you feel?
3. What do you critically say about your 'self'?
4. Does your belief about 'self' oppose God's truth about your 'self?'

....
....
....
....
....

When you are insecure (not secure: not be confident, not safe against attack, not in safe keeping):

1. What do you do to protect yourself?
2. What do you feel?
3. What do you critically say about yourself?
4. Does your belief about 'self' oppose God's truth about your 'self?'

....
....
....
....
....

When you are not feeling significant (do not feel of worth: to have meaning, not to be of real importance):

1. What do you do to protect yourself?
2. What do you feel?
3. What do you say about yourself?
4. Does your belief about 'self' oppose God's truth about your 'self?'

....
....
....
....
....

Exercise task 10

To challenge self-critical thinking consider a recent crisis event when you were at risk of feeling not accepted, not secure, or not significant. How did you protect your 'self'?

What was the situation? What where you doing when you began to feel bad?

....
....
....
....
....

What thoughts / images did you have about the situation / event?

....
....
....
....
....

How did it make you feel emotionally?

....
....
....
....
....

What self-critical thoughts or internal commentary did you have about yourself? (Thoughts, words, images, meanings).

....
....
....
....
....

What did you do to protect yourself?

....
....
....
....
....

Did your thoughts oppose the truth of what God says about you?

....
....
....
....
....

For many of us, our response will be a learned habitual reaction as a consequence of early childhood experiences or due to later life trauma, hence it becoming a possible stronghold.

The following questions may help you to challenge your self-critical, unhelpful thoughts.

- What evidence is my self-critical thought based on?

- Is there an alternative way of looking at my self-critical / unhelpful thinking?

- What is the advantage / disadvantage of my self-critical thinking?

- What is the evidence AGAINST my self-critical thinking? Am I ignoring any positives?

- What would a friend / loving family member say to me?

- Am I applying negative thinking styles to my 'self', biased thinking styles, biased self-perception, biased interpretation, biased self-prejudice?

- Is my self-critical thinking helpful or destructive toward self?

- Is my self-critical thinking standing against the truth of what God says about me?

Rebalancing 'self' critical thought(s): daily combat against self-critical thoughts

Once you have started to identify and challenge your unhelpful self-critical thoughts it is important to re-align them with the truth about your identity to re-balance the negative thinking.

Consider how much your regular negative words / commentary against 'self' have become un-noticed and automatic.

How much do they weigh you down and affect your identity: 'who am I?'

Exercise task 11

To enable a re-balancing of the self- critical thought consider Exercise task 8 and the question:

What self-critical thoughts or internal commentary did you have about yourself? (Thoughts, words, images, meanings.)

....

....
....
....
....

Now use the previous questions to start to re-balance your answer:

- What evidence is my self-critical thought based on?
- Is there an alternative way of looking at my self-critical / unhelpful thinking?
- What is the advantage / disadvantage of my self-critical thinking?
- What is the evidence AGAINST my self-critical thinking? Am I ignoring any positives?
- What would a friend / loving family member say to me?
- Am I applying negative thinking styles to my 'self': biased thinking styles, biased self-perception, biased interpretation, biased self-prejudice?
- Is my self-critical thinking helpful or destructive toward self?
- Is my self-critical thinking standing against the truth of what God say about me?

Re-balanced thought may be:

....
....
....
....
....

Review the re-balanced thought in the table below:

Unhelpful/ critical thought	Re-balanced thought

To further re-balance your self-critical thinking so that it is truth based rather than fear based, try writing three columns:

- One for the self-critical thought

- One for the balanced thought (Use the previous questions to help find the balanced thought)

- One for the truth (of how God perceives you).

Example:

Self-critical thought	Balanced thought	Thought based on truth
No one ever includes me	I have been invited to some parties and because I am not invited does not mean I am not liked or significant.	God loves me. He chose me and adopted me. I am part of His family. Ephesians 1:4-5

This is a process of renewing the mind, or re-thinking identity. *Romans 12:2*

It is important to remember that as we *identify, challenge and re-balance* self-critical thinking, our emotional well-being, daily living activities (behavioural responses: what we do) and relationships (with self, others and God) will be affected.

For example: notice how the difficult emotion changes as the thought is re-balanced with the truth. This is renewing of the mind, which results in a re-thinking of identity.

Difficult emotion	Self-critical thought	Balanced thought	Thought based on truth	New emotion
Rejection Sadness Self-pity	No one ever includes me	I have been invited to some parties and because I am not invited does not mean I am not liked or significant.	God loves me. He chose me and adopted me. I am part of His family. Ephesians 1:4-5	Peaceful Loved Accepted

As old habitual ways of thinking are identified, challenged and rebalanced we will re-think identity of 'self' and our emotional and behavioural responses will change. This is a process and a journey.

Exercise task 12

Over the next week keep a journal as you take steps to identify, challenge and re-balance your critical thinking about 'self'. You may want to use a record sheet so that you can map your progress of change over a period of time.

It may initially feel difficult to employ the re-thinking process, but remember you may have created a habit pattern (stronghold/s) of self-critical thoughts, so be patient and kind to your 'self'!

Difficult Emotion	Self-criticall Thought	Balanced Thought	Thought based on Truth (God's words	New Emotional Response	New behavioural response (what you do, how you relate to others)
Guilt, self-rejection	It is all my fault, I always get it wrong.	This is all or nothing thinking. I'm not completely to blame. If I made a mistake I can say sorry.	God loves me and rejoices over me. We all make mistakes, this does not make me a loser.	Freedom No longer fearful	I don't have to hide away and withdraw but can be honest and open about my mistake.

Truth cards

Once you have found a more realistic and truth based statement about your 'self' it may be helpful to write down the statement on a small card. Whenever you start to be critical of your 'self' in your thinking, your 'truth card' will remind you of the truth concerning your identity.

For example you may want truth cards with:

- The questions used to challenge the self-critical thoughts.

- Biblical truths written on them of who you are 'in Christ'.

- Your balanced thoughts written on them.

For example: Some of the questions used to challenge the self-critical thoughts can be placed on the card and put in your pocket as a reminder to challenge your self-critical thinking.

TRUTH CARD

- What evidence is my self-critical thought based on?

- Is there an alternative way of looking at my self-critical / unhelpful thinking?

- What is the advantage / disadvantage of my self-critical thinking?

- What is the evidence AGAINST my self-critical thinking? Am I ignoring any positives?

- What would a friend / loving family member say to me?

Looking back at Module 1 create truth cards with statements about the truth of your identity: who you are 'in Christ'.

For example:

BIBLICAL TRUTH CARD

I have been chosen by God and adopted as his child. Ephesians 1:4 and 5

Truth card with your balanced thought written on them.

TRUTH CARD

I don't have to prove myself. I don't need to strive to achieve. It is ok if I make a mistake: everyone does. I am significant.

The importance of speaking truth to self and receiving truth.

We have established that habitual negative words, the self-critical commentary, will often become un-noticed and automatic. The Self-critical commentary maintains low self-evaluation and can significantly affect identity and the answer to the 'who am I?' question.

Speaking truth to 'self' breaks the vicious cycle of self-critical thinking and what the psychologist Christine Padesky describes as being 'prejudiced against self'. To further reset the internal scales of thinking it is helpful to start to acknowledge the truth of who we are 'in Christ' and to learn to appreciate the 'self': personal positive qualities, emotions and actions. Indeed it is important to commence the process of loving 'myself' and then loving my neighbour.

Exercise task 13

As part of resetting the internal scales of the prejudiced attitude against your 'self,' start to make a list of your positive qualities.

This may be difficult at first and you may need to challenge the significant voices of earlier experiences:

- Culture - so often the message heard is that it is wrong and proud to state our personal positive qualities: 'who do you think you are?' Additionally there may be a significant family voice that may discourage your efforts: 'we (Family name) ...., will never amount to much.'
- It may be that the significant adults in your life did not praise or encourage you.
- It may be that a later life trauma has undermined your self-evaluation.

To help identify your positive qualities list, consider:

- Do you value your 'self' as God values you?
- What do other people like or value in you: ask a friend!
- How might another person who cares about you describe you?
- What qualities do you value in others that you share? (Someone who is kind / listens etc.)

- What gifts or talents do you have, however modest? (I am good at maths / swimming / remembering / washing dishes / talking to people etc.)
- As you consider the challenges that you have faced in your life (e.g., illness, bereavement, divorce, neglect, etc.) what strengths can you identify in your 'self'?
- What positive qualities do you have? (I am kind, thoughtful etc.)
- What do you like about yourself? (I am good at... / I enjoy... / I help others by... / I have overcome... etc.)

My positive qualities and strengths are:

....

....

....

....

....

Exercise task 14

As part of learning to break the cycle of self-critical thinking and our prejudiced thoughts against 'self,' it is important to learn to express positive feelings. This will include the giving and receiving of compliments rather than dismissing them, which maintains the negative cycle of ignoring disconfirming truth.

For a period of time keep a compliments diary. Note down:

A. When you were paid a compliment.
B. Be alert to not dismissing or deflecting the compliment or the person who made it.
C. Acknowledge, accept and agree with the compliment. *E.g. 'Thank you very much, I'm pleased with how it turned out.'*
D. When giving a compliment be clear and specific. *E.g. 'That was a delicious meal.'*

CASE EXAMPLE - Keisha

Keisha had been married for 3 years and had a little boy of 11months. Keisha was struggling in her marriage and while attending counselling she was exploring what it meant for her to find her significance in relation to God and what it meant to love her 'self.'

"I realised that I was not seeing myself through God's eyes, that I had lost my 'self' in other people. I was constantly affected by what others said or thought of me. I have started to realise that it is not ok for people to put me down or for me to put myself down. I'm learning that I can accept my 'self' and can forgive 'self' for my mistakes. I can dare to dream and dare to believe the best about my 'self.' I can be patient and kind to my 'self' and allow 'self' to be loved and let my walls come down.

I realise that I have not been doing this and how 'self' critical I have been. It is as though the counselling has 'shone a lot of light' on my thoughts and made me realise that a lot of my thoughts tend to be negative, dwelling on things I'm not doing right or could do better. It is not healthy the way I have dismissed my qualities. I do have something to give. God sees me in a different way and I have gone against how He sees me: 'I'm rubbish, I'm a failure, I've not done ...' God doesn't see me that way. It is really freeing. I have been speaking the truth out loud of how God sees me, I'm not going to let people devalue me. I do have a choice and I do have a say. I can say, 'no I'm not going to take that'. It feels good, it previously felt hopeless. I felt I had to go along with it, but I don't. I can have a relationship.

For the first time I have understood that I have a choice not to believe the lies spoken against me. I am worth a lot and if to no one else, I am of worth to God. I don't need to let the negative sink in. Water off a ducks back. I'm learning to challenge Stewart in a calm clear way: "This is how your behaviour makes me feel. It is not right or true."

I am now respecting my own intrinsic worth, it disarms my anger and is changing my behaviour and mood.

Re-thinking identity is a process, it is a journey of recovery, and just like Keisha's it will involve understanding low self-esteem. To tell your personal narrative to someone helps break the denial and perhaps the secrecy about your low 'self' evaluation. Breaking the silence and prayerfully talking to God about how low self-esteem affects your daily life and relationships, will enable you to start to consider the consequences of your negative thinking on your emotions, physiological and behaviour responses, and indeed your relationship with God.

Re-thinking identity involves renewing the mind and re-thinking and reviewing thought strategies. Awareness of how we think is a key to our self-evaluation and the answer to the 'who am I?' question.

'Be careful how you think, your life is shaped by your thoughts.' *Proverbs 4:23* (Good News Translation)

It is important to learn to identify our negative thinking and to commence the renewing, re-thinking process by changing our negative thinking for truthful thinking. This will include repentance for our self-critical thoughts and for judgments against 'self'. It will take us on a journey of recovery as we learn the biblical truths of how God perceives our identity.

Like Keisha, when we have a low evaluation of 'self', we knowingly and sometimes unknowingly self-sabotage opportunities and / or relationships by using avoidant and safety behaviours to try and protect ourselves from hurt. Keisha would constantly adapt her behaviours, just like a chameleon, in order to fit in, but in fact she was losing her sense of 'self'. Over time this maintained the cycle of low self-esteem; the 'who am I?' became a blur.

We are all of intrinsic worth. We are all made in the image of God and an increasingly healthy evaluation of 'self' depends on our knowledge of how God perceives us. He is the source of our true identity, providing a sense of 'self' and a healthy well-being.

A healthy self-esteem is the assurance of our significance, our acceptance, our security 'in Him.'

Isaiah 43 says 'you are precious and honoured in my sight ... because I love you.'

This is a process of re-thinking, renewing and restoring, hence the recovery curve. It is a journey of discovering the true 'self' as we let go of the masks, the facades, the self-made walls of protection. It is a choice to no longer live in the wrong frame of life were the world view so often distorts the truth about our identity. It is a life long journey as we negotiate each life stage with the assurance of how a loving God perceives the one he has made in his likeness.

- Take some time to review your self-critical thoughts and the effect of your self-critical thinking on your emotional and behavioural responses. How does your self-critical thinking affect your relationships?

- Take time to consider what it means to take captive self-critical thoughts and destroy negative strongholds.

- Make some truth cards to help the process of daily combating self-critical thoughts.

- Be intentional in speaking truth to self and in the giving and receiving of compliments.

- What are you going to take away and act on from Module 5?

Summary of module 5

 To be self-critical is the equivalent to having an internal task master that punishes 'self' each time 'self' does not perform or achieve a certain standard. These standards are of our own making or those of others.

 Self-critical thinking is harmful and hurtful to 'self.' It is a form of grumbling against the 'self' that can eventually be, if it becomes habitual, deadly to the 'true-self'. Self-criticism keeps the 'self' in the 'shadow-lands'.

 The module has looked at how to become aware of self-critical thinking by learning to:

a) Identify 'self' critical thought(s).

b) Challenge 'self' critical thought(s): taking captive self-critical thoughts and destroying negative strongholds.

c) Rebalance 'self' critical thought(s), including daily combat against self-critical thoughts.

⅋ The module has considered the use of truth cards as a tool to enable the re-thinking of identity.

⅋ As part of re-setting the internal scales of the prejudiced attitude against your 'self,' the reader has been challenged to start making a list of personal positive qualities.

⅋ The module has explored the importance of speaking truth to 'self' and receiving truth in the form of compliments.

NOTES

Whether you turn to the right or to the left, your ears will hear a voice behind you, saying. 'This is the way; walk in it'.

Isaiah 30:21

Conclusion

I would like to suggest that *'re-thinking who I really am'* is a challenging journey that involves our individual ability to *choose* and to *renew our thought processes.*

As I have journeyed through life and listened to many, I have come to the conclusion that life is not always fair. Difficult times will have been experienced by all. It is at these difficult life junctures that choices are made.

As we view life's journey we can understand why some have become bitter or have ceased to believe that there is a God who loves us. Rob Parsons in his book 'The wisdom house' [25] talks of a Jewish psychiatrist, Victor Frankl, who experienced life in the death camps (Auschwitz and Dachau) in the Holocaust where he lost his wife, his family, his health and saw and experienced deep suffering. Frankl said this:

"Everything can be taken from a man but one thing: the last of the human freedoms - to choose one's attitude in any given set of circumstances, to choose ones' own way."

Our ability to choose can be a powerful agent for change in any given situation. Frankl's counsel is that a different choice can be made, he suggests we can choose another response;

"We can choose not to condemn ourselves to a prison of a thousand 'what if's?' We can chose faith over cynicism. We

---

[25] The Wisdom house by Rob Parsons: Chapter 2 'Life's not fair': page 14.

can choose to affirm that though it is broken and battered, this is still a beautiful world, with endless possibilities for redemption and hope."[26]

We may have lost much but we can still choose how we live tomorrow. We can choose to *re-think who I really am*.

As we have considered the journey of '*re-thinking who I really am*' it is apparent that identity is not defined by status, achievements or commodities.

What we do, what we have achieved, what we own, may explain something about us but they do not define us. Equally, our perceived failures or weaknesses do not define us. They are not our identity.

I believe the ultimate source of a healthy self-esteem is found in relationship with the One who made us. It is not dependent on what we do or on a need to adapt our behaviours in order to earn love, significance or acceptance.

We are a new creation and are becoming whole persons as we come into in the presence of God, focusing on and listening to the words Father God speaks. It is in this place of relationship that the new 'self' is no longer held in captivity by the significant voices that the old 'self' listened to and believed.

Changing the way we think about 'self', others and God involves choice and is a process of renewing the mind, it is a life long journey. God is committed to our life journey. He

---

[26] Man's search for meaning: 3rd edition. (Beacon Press, 1992)

crafted us, completely knows us, fully loves us and in him we find our completeness.

This book, *'re-thinking who I really am'*, has sought to encourage engagement in answering that all important question, so often asked: *'Who am I?'*

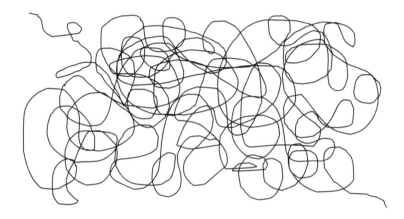

THE 'WHO I AM' CHECK-UP

It is hoped that the book *re-thinking who I really am'* has enabled the reader to take a journey of re-thinking 'self' evaluation, with each module providing stepping stones, tools and strategies to rebuild a true self-identity which may have previously become broken down or distorted.

As life's journey progresses through its many and varied stages and challenges, it is important to regularly pull in at a 'review station' for a check-up and ask that all important question; 'who am I?'

Using what you have learned about your 'self' in relation to your Heavenly Father it may help you to consider the following as part of your *'Who I am?' check-up:*

Reviewing the past month take a moment to consider the following

- On a scale of 0-10 how would you score your present 'self' evaluation?

  (0 being the lowest - 10 being the highest).

0	1	2	3	4	5	6	7	8	9	10

- How would you describe your 'self' using your 'I am' statements:

  I am ....

  I am ....

  I am ....

- Write down your internal negative thought commentary: your typical 'self 'doubting, 'self' critical, comparing 'self ' to others 'self' talk:

  ....
  ....
  ....
  ....
  ....

- Whose significant voices have you been listening to? Have they been helpful (H) or unhelpful (UN)?

  ....   (H)   (UN)

  ....   (H)   (UN)

  ....   (H)   (UN)

- How has your low evaluation of 'self' affected your thoughts, emotions, physical responses, behavioural responses and your relationship with God?

  Thoughts / images:
  ....
  ....
  ....
  ....
  ....

Emotional responses:

....
....
....
....
....

Physical responses:

....
....
....
....
....

Behavioural responses:

....
....
....
....
....

Relationship with God:

....
....
....
....
....

How are you maintaining your low evaluation of 'self'?

- **Biased perception:** bias in how you see your 'self':

  What positive aspects of your 'self' are you ignoring?

  ....
  ....
  ....
  ....
  ....

  How are your biased perceptions affecting your evaluation of 'self'?

  ....
  ....
  ....
  ....
  ....

- **Biased interpretation:** meaning attached to event or circumstance.

  Consider a recent circumstance or event that you viewed negatively. What positives about your 'self' did you dismiss or ignore?

  ....
  ....
  ....
  ....
  ....

  How did your biased interpretation affect your evaluation of 'self'?

  ....
  ....

....
....
....

- **Biased thinking style:**

  Reflect on a recent event or circumstance when your
  estimation of your 'self' was negative. What biased thinking
  style/s were you using?

  ....
  ....
  ....
  ....
  ....

  How did your biased thinking style/s affect your evaluation
  of 'self'?

  ....
  ....
  ....
  ....
  ....

- **Prejudicial thinking:**

  When thinking about a recent event or circumstance were
  your thoughts prejudicial against your 'self'.

  Write down some of your negative beliefs held against your
  'self'. Note whether these thoughts were helpful or
  unhelpful.

  ....
  ....
  ....
  ....
  ....

How did your prejudicial thinking affect your evaluation of 'self'?

....
....
....
....
....

- **Rules for living / assumptions:**

  Whilst reflecting on a recent event or circumstance note what rules you were applying to your 'self':

  I must ....

  I ought to ....

  I should ....

  What assumptions were you applying to 'self'?

  If I do .... ,
  then ....

  How did these rules and assumptions affect your evaluation of 'self'?

  ....

- **Avoidant and safety behaviours:**

  When thinking about a recent event or circumstance what avoidant or safety behaviours did you employ to protect your 'self'?

  ....
  ....
  ....

....

....

How did these behaviours affect your evaluation of 'self'?

....

....

....

....

....

Using the questions from Module 5 what is an alternative re-balanced view of 'self' in the circumstance?

- What evidence is my self-critical thought based on?

- Is there an alternative way of looking at my self-critical / unhelpful thinking?

- What is the advantage / disadvantage of my self-critical thinking?

- What is the evidence against my self-critical thinking? Am I ignoring any positives?

- What would a friend / loving family member say to me?

- Am I applying negative thinking styles to my 'self': biased thinking styles, biased self-perception, biased interpretation, biased self-prejudice?

- Is my self-critical thinking helpful or destructive toward self?

- Is my self-critical thinking standing against the truth of what God say about me?

Re-balanced thought may be:

....
....
....
....
....

As you consider and challenge what 'self' critical thoughts are maintaining your low 'self' evaluation, consider the truth of your core 'I am' baseline identity statements: do they align with the truth of what God says about you?

I am ....

I am ....

I am ....

It is important to recognise that our evaluation of 'self' is a life long journey of discovery in relationship with a loving God who is the source of our being and who brings fullness of life in each life stage. As life is complex there will be undulations and varying seasons, there will be the significant positive and the negative voices. Our core baseline beliefs about 'self' remain increasingly stable as we rest in the truth of our Heavenly Father's significant voice. Ask your 'self'; "What difference does it make to my evaluation of my 'self' to know that I am a child of God?"

He is to be at the centre of our lives. He is God of the past, present and future.

"A poor background does not disqualify us from a great future, or to be used of God powerfully. Everything can change today.

Obviously we want to move out of the dysfunctional behaviour, the key is renewing our thinking". [27]

---

[27] Victorious Mindsets by Steve Backlund

God bless our children and our children's children to know Him and to know who they are 'in Christ'.

Margaret Bristow

About the Author

Margaret is married to Phil and has two daughters and two sons-in-law, who in her eyes are the best!

Margaret enjoys walking by the sea, watching rugby, riding her bike going to the gym and spending quality time with people, especially over a meal. If you asked Margaret what she is passionate about, what would she say? It would be God; seeing people come into greater freedom; for each of us to understand our intrinsic worth and significance; for people to be free from the webs that have entangled them from the past and present.

Margaret originally trained as an Occupational Therapist specialising in mental health, later gaining postgraduate qualifications in Integrative Therapy and Cognitive Behaviour Therapy. Margaret has lived and worked for Christian charities in Pakistan and Hong Kong and now lives in Birmingham where she works as a counsellor and mentor and loves to teach at women's events and church.

Margaret has written 2 (course) books: 're-thinking anxiety' and 're-thinking who I really am'.

Also by same Author

Rethinking Anxiety: A practical guide to deafeating Anxiety

ISBN-13: 978-0956334220

Made in the USA
Charleston, SC
30 May 2016